The Government and Management of Schools

The Government and Management of Schools

GEORGE BARON
and
D. A. HOWELL

THE ATHLONE PRESS *of the University of London*
1974

Published by
THE ATHLONE PRESS
UNIVERSITY OF LONDON
at 4 *Gower Street, London* WC1

Distributed by
Tiptree Book Services Ltd
Tiptree, Essex

U.S.A. and Canada
Humanities Press Inc
New York

© *George Baron and D. A. Howell* 1974

ISBN 0 485 11142 X

Printed in Great Britain by
W & J MACKAY LIMITED, CHATHAM

Preface

The conviction that the school in England is more than an instrumental unit within the educational system is one which has been given precise administrative form in Sections 17 to 21 of the Education Act, 1944. These provide for each school to have its own instruments and articles (or 'rules', as the latter are termed in the case of primary schools). Through these instruments and articles or rules it is associated with a body of individuals who are formally charged with some aspects of its administration and its general conduct. These individuals are school managers or governors. In a large authority they are numbered in their thousands. Every afternoon and every evening hundreds of meetings take place up and down the country in which they, with education officers and heads, discuss the affairs of individual schools, interview candidates for appointment and receive and comment on the reports they receive.

But what is the significance of all this activity? What are its historical antecedents? What part do managers and governors play in the local administration of education? What views are held of their functions by those participating? What different forms do managing and governing bodies take in different types of authority? How are their members chosen? What changes are called for?

It was to seek the answers to these and related questions that a detailed and exhaustive study was carried out within the Department of Educational Administration of the University of London Institute of Education from September 1965 to April 1969. This study was financed by a grant from the Department of Education and Science, whose support and interest is acknowledged with gratitude; and an earlier version of some of the chapters in the present book (especially Chapters 1-4 and 8) forms part of the authors' evidence to the Royal Commission on Local Government in England and Wales, published as Research Study No. 6 (H.M.S.O. 1968). Material derived from this research study is included with the kind permission of the Controller of Her Majesty's Stationery Office. Some parts of Chapter 6 are based on D. A. Howell's evidence to the Central Advisory Council report *Children and their Primary Schools*, which was published as Appendix XIII in Vol. II of that report.

There is one final point to be made. Since the field work for this study was completed there have been changes in attitudes with regards to several aspects of school management and government and a number of authorities have modified their practices, some radically. In particular there has been an increasing acceptance of parents and teachers as managers and governors, and even moves to bring senior pupils on to the governing bodies of secondary schools. But we did not feel that we should attempt to revise findings and judgments arrived at as the result of very full investigations and case studies. On the contrary we felt that to present our findings without any 'retouching' will provide the best basis for a complete evaluation of recent changes when these have had time to demonstrate their influence.

December 1972

G.B.
D.A.H.

Consultations and Acknowledgements

Officers of the following organizations were consulted in the course of the Unit's research: Association of Chief Education Officers; Association of Education Committees; Association of Municipal Corporations; County Councils' Association; National Association of Divisional Executives for Education; National and Local Government Officers' Association; Royal Institute of Public Administration; Confederation of Associations for the Advancement of State Association, and several local Associations; Cheshire Federation of Parent-Teacher Associations; Church of England Schools' Council; Catholic Education Council; Schools Branch and Legal Branch, Department of Education and Science; Central Advisory Council for Education; The Registrars of all English Universities; National Union of Teachers; National Association of Head Teachers; Association of Headmistresses, Headmasters Association; Headmasters Conference, Governing Bodies' Association.

We wish to acknowledge the help given by the following in the planning and the execution of the study: (The posts and titles mentioned are those held at the time.) Dr J. J. B. Dempster, C.E.O., Southampton; Mr H. K. Fowler, Deputy E.O. Herts; Mr F. J. Hill, C.E.O. West Suffolk; Mr H. V. Lightfoot, Director of Education, Newcastle-on-Tyne; Mr J. L. Longland, Director of Education, Derbyshire; Dr J. S. Wilkie, Deputy E.O. Newham; Mr R. M. Gordon, A.E.O., I.L.E.A. and his colleagues at the Divisional Offices; Mr J. L. Sharpe and Mr B. Wood, Royal Commission on Local Government; Mr M. Kogan, Secretary, Central Advisory Council for Education; Prof. H. Maddick and his colleagues at the Institute of Local Government Studies, Birmingham University; Prof J. A. G. Griffith, London School of Economics; Dr R. A. Parker, London School of Economics; Mr W. H. Perkins, formerly Director of Education, Warwickshire; Dr P. G. Richards, Southampton University; Prof W. Taylor, University of Bristol; Prof A. Tropp, University of Surrey.

Officers of the following organizations were consulted with regard to the Unit's evidence to the Public Schools' Commission: Governing Bodies' Association; Association of Governing Bodies of Girls' Public Schools; Girls Public Day School Trust; National Association of Governing Bodies of Aided Grammar Schools; Public Schools Bursars' Association.

We wish to acknowledge the help given by Mr G. F. Cockerell, Secretary to the Commission, and by Dr L. J. Stroud.

We must also acknowledge the ready co-operation of all those whom we sought to interview, and who must remain anonymous. These include Heads, Chairmen of Governing Bodies and other Governors, Chief Education Officers and their colleagues, members of Local Education Authorities and Clerks and Secretaries to Foundations. We owe a special debt to those who were involved in the planning of our area studies.

We end by thanking numerous colleagues at the Institute of Education for their interest and advice; and by acknowledging the substantial help given during the course of the study by our colleagues Miss Jane Tatum, Mr J. I. Gleisner, Miss Deborah Halpin, Miss Marian Hargreaves and Mr Simon Jenkins.

Contents

1 Introduction

There are a number of factors which make a reassessment of school government important at the present time. The first is the assumption, held by the Department of Education and Science and by such bodies as the Association of Education Committees, that with the coming of many larger local authorities, there is need for more responsibility to be exercised at school level. The second is the trend, marked over the past decade, towards the enhancement of the powers and status of the governing bodies of colleges of education and of larger technical colleges. The third is the demand made by a small but influential series of groups, ranging from active parent teacher associations to the bodies brought together in the Home and School Council, for greater lay (and especially parental) participation in the running of the schools. Such participation, supported by the recommendations of the Plowden Report and by various Departmental utterances, takes the form of cooperative work within the schools themselves, as well as representation on managing and governing bodies. The main impetus seems to come from the rapidly growing numbers of people in the professional and managerial classes who rely on the publicly provided system for the education of their children. It is particularly strong at the primary school level. The fourth factor, though certainly not the least in importance, is the growing impatience of the teachers who feel that they are better qualified to contribute to the government of their schools than many representatives of other interests.

Clearly all four factors present a challenge to the governing body (or the managing body) as a minor element in the committee structure of a local education authority, with severely limited activities and with a closely guarded membership. Often it serves no purpose other than that of associating councillors and a few others with the externals of school administration. Can it be brought to satisfy new demands? Is it to continue to be in essence administrative or can it find a role, like that accorded to local councils in the Redcliffe-Maud report, of a mainly advisory character?

These are the questions with which this book and the research on which it is based are concerned. They are questions, too, to which answers are being sought with growing insistency by increasing numbers of teachers, parents, officers and members of the general public. Schools, and how they are run, matter more than ever before and this concern is linked with a general movement towards more widespread participation in the control of educational institutions of all kinds.

In some respects schools are unique institutions, which do not fit easily into the national or the local government structures. They are situated in the border zone between professional, administrative and political authority and in their government there must be a constant tension between these. Any study such as this must therefore be concerned with general issues of the control of major institutions in a democratic society.

It is therefore worth considering the way in which ideas about institutional government have evolved. The earliest is that of trusteeship, by which a group of ostensibly reliable citizens were charged with carrying out the wishes of a founder. Schools, colleges, hospitals, charitable institutions and foundations for many purposes emerge, from the early middle ages onwards, as self-sufficient entities, their existence guaranteed by small groups of men whose main purpose was to safeguard the wealth that made their continuance possible.

From the middle of the seventeenth century new concepts of institutional government began to develop. The growth of commerce and banking, the beginnings of modern investment and the decline in the importance of land as the sole guarantee of permanence all began to militate against the static idea of trusteeship. Subscriptions and fees became standard means of financing schools and supplemented or replaced endowments. The static role of the *trustee* was replaced by that of the *governor*, charged with the dynamic task of regulating the use of resources and with responsibility for the purposes it served.

In the elementary schools that developed as a result of voluntary effort in the early nineteenth century, the *manager* had a related but distinctive role. He was similarly responsible for financial matters and for the proper use of property and monies entrusted to him by the organization which he served or by the government; but he was also responsible in detail for the actual management and day to day conduct of the school and for the work of its teachers. His duties and responsibilities were what now would be termed administrative and are, indeed, carried out by administrative officers.

With the coming of school boards and later of local education authorities still other approaches to school management and government emerge. Schools are now seen as the concern, at local level, of what Birch has termed 'representative and responsible' government.[1] This means that they are controlled by elected representatives of the community, ultimately responsible for all aspects of their work and conduct. Moreover, they are increasingly regarded as units in local school systems, and many of the original functions of managing and governing bodies are vested in education committees and their corps of administrative officers and inspectors.

Nevertheless, the conviction that the school is more than a mere unit in a system has survived and has, indeed, been strengthened by conflicts over individual schools arising in the course of the reorganization of secondary education. Although governors have lost their original final authority, they still express the firmly held assumptions that:

Each school should have associated with it a body of interested and informed men and women, concerned with it as an individual institution.

[1] Birch, A. H., *Representative and Responsible Government*, Allen & Unwin, 1964.

Among these men and women there should be some representing the local education authority (whether council or committee members or not), some appointed by other bodies, such as universities, and some coopted by reason of their educational or other qualifications. Furthermore, among the members, there should be some who can represent the interests of parents, of teachers and of local commerce and industry.

In conjunction with the local education authority and its officers, and with the head of the school, the governing body so constituted should share the responsibility for the making of appointments, for the general conduct of the school and control of curriculum, for the preparation of estimates and for representing the school in issues of importance.

The extent to which these assumptions are translated into reality varies greatly from one local education authority to another, and it is one of the purposes of this study to examine and explain this diversity. It exists at a time when there appears to be the beginnings of another shift of emphasis in the control of educational institutions. There has developed a widely diffused sentiment that it is not enough for schools and colleges to be governed by a limited number of elected representatives: instead, it is argued that *representativeness* and *responsibility* need to be diffused as widely as possible throughout the social structure, if democratic government is to be achieved. This means that there must be as full and varied opportunities as possible for large numbers of people to assist in the formation of opinion, to trace the course of decision-making, to take part in resulting action and to evaluate its results. It follows that not only the formally designated representatives of the community but those who work in, or are clients of, publicly provided institutions should also have a say in their affairs.

'Participation' may at present be a catch-phrase devoid of precise significance. Even so it embodies an important principle, namely that the effectiveness of a democratic society can be measured by the provision it makes for the ordinary man or woman to take part in the control of its institutions. It is clearly capable of being realized in the local government of education, if only because the clients, whether parents, employers, citizens or students have knowledge of the working of the services provided and are near to the agencies of control, in a psychological as well as a physical sense. This proximity gives scope for improving the quality of communication in both directions. Committee members and officers can consult with and listen to teachers, parents and governors, while the latter can, by reason of both general and specific knowledge, directly or indirectly contribute to policy formation. This initiative may develop at any point in the system. The extent to which governors can play a part in such a pattern of action and interaction is one measure of their effectiveness.

A governing body can, on the one hand, be envisaged as the extension of the national and local *system* of education to the individual unit, the *school*. On the other it can be seen as an essential part of the school itself viewed as an institution. If the first approach is dominant the purposes of the school are determined by inspectors or administrative officers, who occupy a superior position in a well-defined hierarchy in relation to heads and teachers. Lay responsibility only manifests itself in formal terms at the pinnacle of the structure, as in the School Board in the United States or in the State Legislature in Australia. Decisions in the vital areas of appointment of staff and curriculum are the concern of the system, and are the subject of universally applied and carefully prescribed regulations. The principal or head is above all a public servant, operating within a bureaucratic context. If the second approach is dominant decision-making is a matter for the individual school. The local authority or other body that controls the provision of education in an area and the officers who serve it are regarded as having a limited role, which embraces the acquisition and distribution of resources, but not the detailed determination of their use. Thus there is a wide range of *professional* responsibilities, such as the grouping of pupils, the selection of examinations for them to sit, the choice of texts and schemes of work, the appointment of staff and their allocation to duties within the school and the organization of non-academic activities, which are held to be the concern of the head and his staff. In such cases, however, since schools are public institutions, there is a conviction, or at least an acceptance, that very close to the school there should be some body representative of the public interest.

In any educational system both approaches are to be found and in England the tension between the two is particularly marked. Because of the prominence and influence of the major independent Public Schools, and the necessarily individual character of voluntary schools which, whether Anglican or Catholic, depend in part upon local exertions, the school is credited with an individuality which is elsewhere only attributed to some institutions of higher education. There is, indeed, a constant striving on the part of heads to emphasize and extend the freedom they enjoy from local authority control and the status of a school varies directly with the degree of success achieved in this direction. For this reason, there are attractions in the idea of a governing body as a means of providing some visible guarantee of a school's individuality.

It is easy to appreciate the place of governors in the independent school world. There must be a body of persons responsible for the finances and material assets of the school, for the appointment, dismissal and remuneration of its staff and for the continuity of its traditions and character. Such a body, however, does not normally concern itself with professional matters, which are left to the headmaster.

It is easy, too, to appreciate the place of managers and governors in all that concerns voluntary schools. Certain rights and duties (notably those concerned with the appointment of staff and religious instruction), are accorded by legislation to schools originating from voluntary effort within both Anglican and Catholic communities. There must be a body of persons in each case who can discharge such duties and rights, at least in times of emergency.

The place of managers and governors for individual schools which are collectively the responsibility of local education authorities is less easy to assess. Although in recent years they have been much discussed, there has been no research, other than that on which this book is based, into the forms they take and the purposes they serve.

Similarly, there is no body of theory relating to educational administration that can serve to underpin this study. There are a considerable number of assumptions accumulated over the years concerning the separation of 'administration' and teaching, the place of the head, the freedom of the teacher and the relationships of central and local authorities, but they are useful guidelines for the administrator, rather than a connected body of theory as such. But there is no reason why they should not be eventually submitted to examination, and the study of school government provides a useful starting-point.

The organization and methodology of the research on which this book is based are described in an appendix. It is sufficient here to say that means had to be devised to map and analyse a very great variety of structures, practices, assumptions and rationalizations. It was essential therefore to carry out extensive exploratory field work. During the four years covered by the research, every local education authority in England save one was visited by a member of the unit and many hundreds of heads, administrative officers and councillors, managers and governors were interviewed. In addition much help was received from local government and educational associations and from individuals with especial knowledge of educational administration. These direct contacts were supplemented by questionnaire studies, which brought us into touch with the experience and views of nearly two thousand heads and governors.

The research project, like this book, was centred on the governing bodies of county secondary schools. But it also included substantial studies of the management of primary schools, independent schools and direct grant schools. It thus covered all main aspects of the total school structure.

2 The Historical Background

THE MANAGEMENT OF ELEMENTARY SCHOOLS

When public money was first made available for elementary education in the form of building grants in 1833, there were no administrative structures through which it could be channelled. It had therefore to be entrusted, following recommendation by one of the two great voluntary societies,[1] to groups of citizens who had made themselves responsible for setting up and maintaining schools. In practice, however, day-to-day management of schools normally fell to local clergymen or active members of the nonconformist churches.

One of the aims of Kay-Shuttleworth when he was appointed Secretary of the Committee of Council on Education in 1839 was to enable laymen to take a greater part in the management of schools. From 1833 to 1839 the whole responsibility for determining the constitution of church schools had rested with the founders. In the Committee's Minutes of 1839-40 specimen trust deeds were suggested for adoption, and in 1847 acceptance of prescribed management clauses by all church schools given building grants was made a condition of such grants. Kay-Shuttleworth's proposals that each school should have a board responsible for the management of the school (moral and religious instruction being entrusted to the clergy) met with opposition from the National Society,[2] but they served to emphasize the principle that school management was a matter for lay participation. (At a later period

[1] That is, the National Society, founded in 1811 and the British and Foreign Schools Society, founded in 1814.

[2] *Minutes of the Committee of Council on Education*, Vol. I, pp. 33-34; *Supplementary Minutes*, 10 July 1847; *Minutes*, 1847, Vol. I; and *Minutes*, 1848-9.

similar conditions were imposed for Wesleyan, Roman Catholic, Jewish and undenominational schools.)

Despite the principle of control by committee, it was more often than not the clergyman who had most to do with the everyday administration of the school. He engaged and dismissed teachers, kept such accounts as were necessary, saw to the maintenance and repair of school property, supervised the instruction and often shared in it himself, and was intimately concerned with the discipline and welfare of individual children. With the setting up of school boards after 1870 close concern with the details of management by lay people proved possible in small rural boards and boards with only one or two schools, but in the larger (and principally urban) boards the emergence of officers, inspectors and clerks to carry out administrative duties lessened the need for lay managers. Most of the large boards, for example, Birmingham, Manchester, Leeds, Bradford and Hull,[3] preferred to administer their schools centrally rather than delegate duties to bodies of managers as they were permitted to do under the Elementary Education Acts. Two notable exceptions to central management were London and Liverpool.[4] In London each board school had associated with it a body of managers who seem in many cases to have visited it with assiduity, interested themselves in what was taught, were concerned with the welfare of both teachers and pupils, inspected attendance records and took part in the social occasions that were already a feature of elementary school life.[5] In Liverpool the entire duty of management was remitted to bodies of local managers.

The Cross Commission in its enquiry into elementary education saw school administration as having two aspects:[6] the first was concerned with providing buildings, money and equipment, and with complying with the law; the second was concerned with the daily routine and work of the school, with the teachers and

---

[3] *Cross Commission*, 1888, *Report*, Part III, Chapter 3, pp. 68–9.
[4] Ibid., pp. 68–9.
[5] Spalding, T. A., *The Work of the London School Board*, 1900, pp. 109–13.
[6] *Cross Commission*, 1888, *Report*, Part III, Chapter 3, and Part VII, p. 209.

children and with the life of the neighbourhood. In the case of voluntary schools and school districts with only a few board schools these two aspects of management might well be combined, but in the larger school boards the Commission recommended that they be kept separate. For the first aspect the school board was thought to be the right instrument, but for the second it was essential that there should be a group of responsible individuals associated with the school.

After 1902 the Local Education Authorities set up by the Education Act had the duty of maintaining and keeping efficient all public elementary schools. Managing bodies were prescribed only for voluntary schools and schools provided by county councils; county boroughs and Part III authorities[7] could do as they pleased, and any powers they accorded to managers might be very trivial. In London, however, managers were charged with drawing up an annual report, checking school records, inspecting premises and equipment, advising on the appointment of staff, investigating complaints against teachers, promoting visits of educational value and helping in arrangements for school meals, play centres, school savings banks and school open days.[8]

Voluntary schools everywhere continued to have their own managing bodies, although one-third representation of the LEA was required. Voluntary school managers retained complete control over religious instruction and substantial powers over the appointment and dismissal of staff. But after 1902 the control of salaries and finance generally and control over secular education, the curriculum and other aspects of administration lay with the local authority. The local authority also determined the numbers and educational qualifications of the teachers. Thus, in voluntary schools the administrative role of managers was eroded by the expansion of local 'education offices' and the development of statutory health and welfare services.

[7] That is, boroughs and urban districts made responsible under Part III of the Education Act, 1902 for elementary education.

[8] L.C.C. Regulations, 1911: *Managers of Public Elementary Schools* (*Council and Non-Provided*).

The Education Act of 1944, in an attempt to establish a common administrative framework for all primary schools required that *all* should have a body of managers. Voluntary schools continued to have (in the main) individual managing bodies, but the greater financial responsibility assumed by the local authorities was reflected in their constitution and powers.[9] Although county schools were also required to have managers, the individual element could be nullified by the practice of grouping schools for management purposes, a practice very common in county boroughs and not infrequent in counties. Moreover, for both voluntary and county schools, rules of management are framed by the local authority, and managers can thus be left with no effective powers or functions (other than those expressly conferred by the Act and mainly in connection with aided schools).

ENDOWED AND PUBLIC SCHOOLS

To arrive at an understanding of the place that came to be accorded to the governing bodies of secondary schools it is essential to turn to the work of the Public Schools Commission and the Schools Inquiry Commission, whose activities extended from 1861 to 1868. The Public School Commissioners were faced with bringing some kind of administrative order into the exceedingly involved affairs of nine major public schools. Their problem, in the main, was that of defining the proper spheres of decision of two kinds of authority: the authority of trustees and governors acting in the public interest, and the authority of the headmaster derived from a narrow but well understood academic tradition. In some cases governors exercised influence over the teaching in a school, and over its day-to-day organization; in others head-

[9] A *controlled* primary school has one-third foundation managers to two-thirds LEA/minor local authority members. Foundation managers retain certain rights over religious instruction in the school and the appointment of some teachers. An *aided* primary school has two-thirds foundation managers to one-third LEA/minor local authority managers. Managers retain control over religious instruction and the appointment of teachers; and they are responsible for certain external repairs and alterations to the school building.

masters virtually took over the functions of governors, selling and buying property on behalf of the school, fixing and receiving school fees and launching and following through ambitious schemes of school building.

In their final report the Commissioners considered that there were some features common to the governing body of a great public school:[10]

Such a body should be permanent in itself, being the guardian and trustee of the permanent interests of the School: though not unduly large, it should be protected by its numbers and by the position and character of its individual members from the domination of personal or local interests, or personal or professional influences or prejudices; and . . . should . . . include men conversant with the world, with the requirements of active life, and with the progress of literature and letters.

The Commissioners recommended that clear lines should be drawn between the functions of governors and headmaster.[11]

The powers of the governors

should include, at the least, the management of the property of the school, and of its revenue, from whatever source derived; and the control of its expenditure; the appointment and dismissal of the Head Master, the regulation of the boarding-houses, of fees and charges, of Masters' stipends, of the terms of admission to the school, and of the times and length of the vacations; the supervision of the general treatment of the boys, and all arrangements bearing on the sanitary conditions of the school.

The headmaster was to be 'unfettered' as regards discipline and teaching:

Details, therefore, such as the division of classes, the school-hours, and school books, the holidays and half-holidays during the school time, belong properly to him rather than to the Governing Body; and the appointment and dismissal of Assistant Masters, the measures necessary for maintaining discipline, and the general direction of the course and

10 Public Schools Commission, 1864, *Report* I, p. 5.
11 Ibid., p. 6.

methods of study, which it is his duty to conduct and his business to understand thoroughly, had better be left in his hands.

It was, however, stressed that the curriculum should not be left to the headmaster:

The introduction of a new branch of study or the suppression of one already established, and the relative degrees of weight to be assigned to different branches, are matters respecting which a better judgment is likely to be formed by . . . men conversant with the requirements of public and professional life and acquainted with the general progress of science and literature, than by a single person, however able and accomplished, whose views may be more circumscribed and whose mind is liable to be unduly pressed by difficulties of detail. What should be taught, and what importance should be given to each subject, are therefore questions for the Governing Body; how to teach is a question for the Head Master.

The Schools Inquiry Commission was faced by a much more complex task, since it was charged with looking into the affairs of some five to six hundred endowed and proprietary schools of a baffling variety. In their recommendations on governing bodies the Commissioners pronounced strongly in favour of 'a special body of Trustees with ample but clearly defined powers and complete responsibility of the Master to them.'[12] For the management of a purely day school they suggested a fixed number of co-optative trustees originally selected from the existing trustees; an equal number selected by householders of the town or parish, or in boroughs appointed by the Town Council, or in other places by the local board; and an equal number appointed by the 'Provincial Board'. For boarding schools they recommended that the governing body should consist of appointees of the 'Provincial Board'[13] and others co-opted by the governors themselves.

The headmaster[14] was to be 'assigned all the internal discipline, the choice of books and methods, the organization, and the appointment and dismissal of assistants.' The external government

[12] Schools Inquiry Commission, 1868, Report I, pp. 244–76.
[13] Ibid., p. 645.
[14] Ibid., pp. 617–19.

of the school was to be shared between the proposed provincial authority and the governing body: the governors were to 'determine what subjects should be taught in the school, and what should be their relative importance'. They were also to be responsible for the financial management of the school and for the appointment and dismissal of the headmaster. The provincial authority was to determine the grade of the school (there were to be first, second and third grade schools) and the part it should play in its area (for example, in the provision of boarding education).

The Endowed Schools Commissioners, who had the task of putting the Inquiry's recommendations into practice, followed the recommendations of the Commissioners in defining the respective functions of the governing body and the headmaster. But in respect of the composition of governing bodies they were at once hampered by the failure of the Endowed Schools Act of 1869 to provide for the setting up of 'Provincial Authorities'. They had, indeed, to make new governing bodies as best they could 'out of old materials'. They adopted the principle that 'Variety of composition seems necessary to due healthiness and vigour of action'.[15] But in the absence of provincial authorities they were 'left to supply the elements of continuity, skill and wider interests out of the official and co-optative portions of the Governing Bodies'.

The Royal Commission on Secondary Education which reported in 1895 recommended that secondary education should be brought within the province of local education authorities, but did not think that their supervision could 'be extended generally to the details of administration which form a large part of the duties of the governing body of a school.'[16] They therefore argued that governing bodies should continue in the case of existing endowed schools (with local authority representation) and that governing bodies 'independent, in their own spheres, of the Local Authority' should be instituted for newly founded schools.

No longer was the issue that which had faced the Public Schools and Schools Inquiry Commissioners, namely the revitaliz-

[15] *Endowed Schools Commission*, 1872, *Report*, p. 13.
[16] *Bryce Commission*, 1896, *Report*, p. 157.

ation of the government of old schools; on the contrary, with the coming of the new locally elected local authorities, it was now felt that active governing bodies were means by which established schools could be protected from over-bureaucratic control.

THE BOARD OF EDUCATION AND THE LOCAL AUTHORITIES

This issue became one of practical significance with the passing of the Education Act of 1902. Hitherto, each secondary school had been, in effect, a single administrative unit, responsible for its own finance and continuance. After 1902 local education authorities were able both to take over and aid existing secondary schools and to found new ones. Should all schools, then, be wholly absorbed within the new local government structure and be treated merely as outgrowths of the strictly regimented elementary school system? Or should their individuality be in some way safeguarded?

In the case of new schools built by the local authorities and existing schools taken over by them, full control and management rested with the authorities. But for other secondary schools aided by local authorities no attempt was made in the Act to lay down general rules as to the constitution of governing bodies, especially in respect of local authority representation. However, where local authorities gave aid to schools they usually sought the right to appoint representatives to their governing bodies, in proportion to the amount of aid. The Board of Education, whose concept of education was in the tradition of the public schools and the old grammar schools, strove to achieve some independence for all secondary schools and saw the governing body as an instrument for achieving this aim. Since schools and authorities were dependent upon the Board for grants, the existence of a governing body was woven into the Regulations for Secondary Schools as a condition of recognition of a school for grant purposes.

Some of the new local authorities, however, did not share the Board's belief in the need for governing bodies, especially for schools which they provided. These authorities, and certainly their newly-appointed 'Directors of Education', were faced by endowed grammar schools struggling to maintain their independence and challenge the authority of the officials with whom they had to deal. Many of the latter had little sympathy with the development of the individuality of what they regarded as 'their' schools, or with the personal aspirations of their headmasters and headmistresses but were, on the contrary, very much occupied with creating a firm pattern of administration in their area. Their attitude contrasted and clashed strongly with that of the officials of the Board and its inspectors, who were men educated in schools of national status and prestige and who viewed secondary education as a vehicle of the cultural life and traditions of the nation as a whole rather than for local and sectional interests.[17] The issue of whether a secondary school should be administered directly from the office of a Director of Education, or whether some means could be found for limiting his control and emphasizing the distinctiveness of the functions of head and teaching staff, became one of key significance.

In the Prefatory Memorandum to the Regulations of 1904, Sir Robert Morant, the first Permanent Secretary of the Board of Education, stated that in the case of all schools

the Board attach importance to direct communication with the Govern-

---

[17] The attitude of the Board may be seen in an extract from a Minute by one of its officers concerning secondary schools in Kent (Public Record Office File Ed. 53/103): 'I think it most unfortunate that in compiling these Regulations the County Council have coupled Secondary Schools with Technical Schools and Classes, Continuation Schools and Teachers Classes. Secondary Schools should be treated separately as Institutions sui generis. They are not meant (like technical institutes) to train their Scholars for this or that trade; their object is to give Scholars a sound general training, mental, physical and moral . . . How can we expect that the tone of the great Public Schools which, because of that tone, have been only recently described as amongst England's most cherished possessions, can possibly enter into and permeate these smaller secondary schools if they are governed by such feeble governing bodies as these local committees must necessarily be if they have no powers. The result of these Regulations if allowed will be that the tone of secondary education will be lowered, and all freedom and elasticity will disappear under the pressure of the iron heel of the County Council.'

ing Body, and to preserving for the Governing Body as much responsibility, independence and freedom of action as is consistent with effective control of educational policy and educational provision, by the Local Authority in its own area, and by the Central Authority in all areas.[18]

In the following year Morant urged that a governing body

shall have such powers and be so constituted as to ensure living interest in the School on the part of the Governors, a real supervision by them of the conduct and progress of the School, and ready access to them by the Headmaster,

and that it

shall contain a proportion of members who are qualified by experience of Higher Education to supply well-informed criticism upon, and intelligent encouragement of, the School work.

He went on to state that

Full efficiency can be secured, and the best teaching and organising power attracted, only when the Headmaster or Headmistress is entrusted with a large amount of responsibility for and control over teaching, organisation and discipline. In particular, the appointment and dismissal of the Assistant Staff is a matter in which a voice ought to be secured to the Headmaster[19]

Some Directors of Education continued to be highly reluctant to have an intermediate body between themselves and the schools and were slow to satisfy the Board.[20] Despite pressure by the Board some of the larger authorities continued their defiance, and it was decided that more detailed direction was needed. The Prefatory Memorandum, 1909, stated that

All grant-earning schools are required by Article 22 to have an Instrument of Government approved by the Board. In the case of Endowed

[18] *Regulations for Secondary Schools*, 1904.
[19] *Regulations for Secondary Schools*, 1905.
[20] Birmingham, for example, refused to submit Instruments of Government, and insisted that the Higher Education Sub-Committee was the governing body of the Council's secondary schools and Council pupil teacher centre (Public Record Office File Ed. 53/55).

Schools, this is either the Scheme, or a body of Regulations made under the Scheme. For schools provided by an LEA the Board have drawn up a model form of Articles of Government which embodies all the provisions which the Board require . . . Any alternative form of instrument may be proposed for acceptance which makes satisfactory provision for (a) the composition of the Governing Body; (b) the appointment and dismissal of assistant teachers; (c) the powers and responsibilities of the Headmaster or Headmistress; and (d) the relations of the Governing Body to the LEA in respect of Finance. The Governing Body should be so constituted as to ensure that it shall be in full personal touch with the School, that it shall have time and interest for the effective discharge of its duties, and that it shall not be overloaded with other functions. There shall be secured to the Headmaster or Headmistress a voice in appointment and dismissal of the assistant staff, and a right to submit proposals to, and be consulted by, the Governing Body.[21]

The line of thought pursued by the Board is exemplified in the following quotation:

I firmly believe—I think all the Inspectors share the belief—that Schools benefit by having an instrument of government clearly defining the function of the Governing Body and the Headmaster and the relations between the Governing Body and the Headmaster and staff. I think we are quite strong enough to see such a regulation enforced and as soon as the Legal Branch have settled the Model Form of Regulations for Municipal Schools, we shall be in a position to lend the various local education authorities material assistance in the preparation of governing instruments for the Schools under their direct control. Such instruments would be especially useful in the case of Municipal Schools as tending to prevent the Organizing Secretary from exceeding his proper function, seeing that those positions and functions would be more clearly defined than they can be defined at present without such a governing instrument.[22]

The Model Articles, drawn up and circulated towards the end of 1908, prescribed that each school provided by a local authority

---

[21] Regulations for Secondary Schools, 1909.
[22] Public Record Office File Ed. 12/124, April 1908.

should be governed by a governing body constituted as a sub-committee of the authority's Education Committee. Its duties were to include the preparation of annual estimates, including salary payments and fee income. The Model Articles also state that the governors shall

prescribe the general subjects of instruction, the relative prominence and value to be assigned to each group of subjects, what reports shall be required to be made to them by the Head Master, the arrangements respecting the school terms, vacations and holidays (and the number of boarders, where appropriate). They shall undertake general supervision of the sanitary condition of the school buildings and arrangements. Subject to the provisions of these Articles with respect to the submission and approval of estimates they shall fix the number of Assistant Teachers to be employed, and the amount to be paid for the purpose of providing and maintaining proper school plant or apparatus, and awarding prizes.

The place accorded to the headmaster was delineated with especial care in the following paragraphs:

. . . the Governors shall consult the Head Master in such a manner as to give him full opportunity for the expression of his views, and he shall be entitled to be present at all meetings of the Governors, save when otherwise determined by them at any particular meeting. The Head Master may also from time to time submit proposals to the Governing Body for making or altering rules concerning any matter within the province of the Governors. The Governors shall fully consider any such expression of views or proposals and shall decide upon them.

Subject to any rules prescribed by or under the authority of these Articles, the Head Master shall have under his control the choice of books, the methods of teaching, the arrangement of classes and school hours, and generally the whole internal organization, management and discipline of the School, including the power of expelling pupils from the School or suspending them from attendance for any adequate cause to be judged of by him, but on expelling or suspending any pupil he shall forthwith report the case to the Governors. If an aggregate sum is fixed in the estimate for the maintenance of school land and apparatus and prizes, the Head Master shall determine, subject to the approval of the Governors, in what proportion that sum shall be divided among the various objects, for which it is fixed in the aggregate.[23]

The issue of the Model Articles aroused the determined resistance of some Directors of Education, and especially Graham of Leeds, who argued that Parliament intended local education authorities to have a free hand to manage their own schools in accordance with local requirements and without schemes. In a belligerent memorandum prepared for his Committee and sent to the Board[24] he shrewdly pointed out that

. . . apparently the Board's Model Scheme has been drawn up on the basis of the schemes governing the old type of Grammar School. It appears from the Clauses in the Model Scheme that the officials responsible for the Scheme are unacquainted with the actual working conditions of educational administration under large LEAs.

Graham held that it was particularly undesirable that head teachers should have a statutory right of attending meetings of Committees:

The arrangement, although undesirable, might possibly work where the Governing Body is concerned only with one Board, but where the Governing Body has many Schools under its control (as at Leeds, where there are seven Maintained Secondary Schools), business would be hampered, Teachers' and Committee's time wasted, and slackness might arise in the management of the Schools owing to the absence of the Head Teachers.

The objection at the root of Graham's attitude was that through its Model Articles the Board was seeking to reduce the powers of LEAs by dictating their committee structure and undermining the authority of their senior officials. Thus, in a subsequent letter to the Board, Graham wrote:

Since my return from London I have had an opportunity of seeing my Chairman and important members of my Committee and they scoff at

---

23 Public Record Office File Ed. 53/385.

24 Public Record Office File Ed. 53/385, Memorandum on 'Model Articles of Government' for Secondary Schools Provided by a Local Authority, J. Graham, Director of Education, Leeds, 1909.

the idea of the County Council passing a minute which will vest any right in Headmasters or Headmistresses. This is not done even in principal officers—Town Clerk, Treasurer, myself—it is contrary to all precedent for a Council to confer a right in regard to anything or any servant to go past the responsible man when they have been placed in charge of a Department.[25]

The Leeds authority flatly refused to modify its regulations, particularly its requirement that all communications from the headmaster to the governing body pass through the office of the Director of Education. In a letter to the Board the authority stated that:

The City Council regard as inexpedient and unreasonable the Board's request that the authority and position of their Chief Executive Officer for Education should be weakened in respect of his relations with the Secondary Schools, or that he should be ignored by the Head Masters and Head Mistresses of such Schools. The Council view with disfavour the sentence contained in the Hansard Extract from Mr. Runciman's speech on the Estimates . . . 'The Head Master ought to be the responsible Executive Officer through whom, and after consultation with whom, the responsible Authority act' . . . The City Council are completely at a loss to understand why the Board should make this demand.

The Chief Executive Officer of any Department of the Corporation is the Adviser of the Committee and the Administrator of the work of the Committee of the Corporation responsible for that Department. It is unreasonable and impracticable for the Board to require that other servants within the same Department, appointed and paid by the Council, should be given executive powers as regards their particular branches of work corresponding with those of the Chief Executive Officer. The Board virtually ask the City Council to make their Chief Executive Officer for Education simply a Minute Clerk, although he alone is held responsible for the whole of the educational finance of the City, and for the whole of the administration of the educational policy of the Council.[26]

[25] Public Record Office File Ed. 53/385: J. Graham, Director of Education, Leeds, to the Board, 26 January 1909.

[26] Public Record Office File Ed. 53/385: Chairman of Leeds Education Committee to the Board, 26 October 1909.

The point about communications passing through the office of the Director of Education received full support from Durham, whose Director appears to have been in contact with Graham. The importance the Board attached to the principle that head-masters should have free access to their governing bodies can be seen in the following extract from Morant to the President:

The points outstanding are positively vital for the well-being of the Secondary Schools in Durham County. If this bureaucratic tyranny by the County Officials is not stopped, the whole 'ethos' of the Secondary School is destroyed and, if he does not give way, it seems true that we must simply stop all our grants. I believe that the Chairman, and the more influential members of the Committee, would not for a moment (if Robson[27] were out of the room) desire this, nor even be very keen to hold out for the administrative tyranny proposed by Mr. Robson.[28]

In the case of Durham the Board modified some of its require-ments and a solution was eventually found. In the case of Leeds, however, the Board decided that firm action was necessary since its authority was being seriously threatened by the support Leeds was getting from other large county boroughs. Consequently, grants were withheld for a short time. Ten authorities[29] in all had adopted in their Instruments of Government a clause identical with or similar to that in the Leeds Instrument which explicitly interposed the Director of Education between the head and the governing body. In four cases, however, the Board had inexpli-cably made no objection to the clause and had approved the Instrument without demur. Consequently, letters pressing for amendment or omission of the clause were sent to all ten authori-ties, from which the Board received only one favourable reply.

Although the Board at first strongly resisted Leeds and other

[27] J. L. Robson, Secretary of Higher Education, Durham.
[28] Public Record Office File Ed. 53/52: Morant to President, 27 April 1909.
[29] The ten authorities were: South Shields, Bolton, Manchester, Birmingham, Leeds, Salford, Birkenhead, Bristol, Norwich, Plymouth. Grants were withheld from Leeds, Birkenhead and Bristol (Public Record Office File Ed. 12/138, Note on 'Position with regard to the interposition of the Director of Education or other Education Official between the Headmaster and the Governing Body', 14 Novem-ber 1910).

authorities, up to the point of withholding grants, very soon afterwards it capitulated, with a completeness and a haste that possibly reflected the upheaval occasioned by the affair of the Holmes Circular and the impending transfer of Morant from the Board. In a minute to the President Morant[30] wrote that the Board had slid into a position that it could not maintain; it had criticized what was widely accepted practice, namely the appointment of the Director of Education of a local education authority as clerk to the governing body or bodies of the secondary schools it provided or maintained.[31] Morant argued for the Board insisting that Articles of Government should make explicit the desired relationship between head and governors. He continued:

It is true that the enactment of provisions of this nature in Articles of Government does not necessarily secure in practice any great degree of freedom for the Headmaster, or for the Governing Body . . . and that where a Local Authority or its Director or both intend to domineer, they will be able to do so, whatever the wording of the scheme.

This, however, points . . . not to the futility of attempting to get satisfactory phrases inserted in Articles of Management, but to our certainly getting the insertion of as many such phrases as we can, and particularly of our getting the Authority to commit itself in black and white to statements that its practice is in fact on lines which connote a satisfactory state of things in these respects. It then becomes obviously more difficult for an Authority or its Director to be frequently infringing the arrangements or carrying them out in a spirit contrary to what is conspicuously plain as the intention of the document.[32]

Up to this point it would seem that the Board and Morant had conceived of the governing body of a secondary school as an administrative agency able, if endowed with adequate formal powers, to protect itself and its school against local authorities

---

[30] Public Record Office File Ed. 53/385: Morant to President, 30 March 1911.
[31] Public Record Office File Ed. 12/138: Memorandum of 14 November 1910. It was estimated that for 113 out of 117 provided or municipal schools in county boroughs, for 61 out of 81 such schools in municipal boroughs, and for 59 out of 135 such schools in strictly county council areas, the Director of Education was also correspondent and probably clerk to the governing body.
[32] Public Record Office File Ed. 53/385: Morant to President, 30 March 1911.

and their officers. This concept had to be abandoned little by little as both authorities and officers grew in experience and confidence. But, as regards one basic issue, the Board was making decisive progress. It was being established that the teaching function (especially as exemplified by the headmaster) should not be regarded as merely executive, but as having authority in its own right. The governing body becomes a symbol of the status of a secondary school and of the independence of its headmaster.

THE INTER-WAR YEARS

Examination of Board of Education files, including some of those dealing with individual local education authorities, during the inter-war years, shows little significant development. Whether a school had a governing body or was controlled directly by the authority depended upon its history, its academic and social standing and, of course, any financial resources it held in its own right.

In Lancashire, for example, the Part III authorities served as agencies for administering the secondary schools in their districts. Many such schools were conducted in the premises of former technical schools, and were governed not under Instruments and Articles of Government, but under local regulations. Secondary schools in other parts of the county were normally endowed grammar schools and had, of course, their own Instruments and Articles. The Chief Education Officer of the time, who was a Wykehamist, and a disciple of Morant, was particularly concerned to see that the grammar schools had a fair share of the County's resources, but he had also to keep on good terms with his Part III authorities.

In Warwickshire each of the nine maintained secondary schools operated under Instruments and Articles, the aim being that they should have the same status as the endowed schools. Two schools were clerked directly from the County Education Office; elsewhere the clerk was a local solicitor or accountant, or where a Part III authority was involved, the local Director of Education. One pair of schools had its own clerk, and another used the services of the clerk of a neighbouring independent school; at one school the clerk was chief assistant to the Town Clerk. All schools had their own banking accounts. The degree of financial independence possessed by the maintained schools was not great, but each was given a small scholarship fund to make their status more comparable to that of the endowed schools. Governors were responsible for appointments, but these were subject to confirmation by the education committee.

In the counties, where secondary education was still mainly the concern of endowed schools, new county schools approximated in their government to the old pattern. Elsewhere, and particularly in the large cities, where maintained schools predominated, they were absorbed within the committee structure of the local authority.

The economy campaign of the early twenties favoured this trend. Until this time all secondary schools in receipt of grants had received them directly from the Board of Education, but such grants were invariably and necessarily supplemented by local education authorities. These in turn were able to claim on the Board for a proportion of their total expenditure. Hence, non-maintained schools were getting grants from two sources. It was ultimately ruled that all schools in this position should decide, following conferences between their governing bodies and the local education authority, whether they should become wholly dependent upon the latter or whether they should continue to receive grants from the Board direct.[33]

Thus, for schools which decided to continue to receive grants direct from the Board it was more than ever essential to have governing bodies, since they were less dependent on their local education authorities than before; governing bodies of schools in the other group, however, lost still more of their purely administrative and financial significance. The coming of regular

[33] This did not mean that local education authorities could no longer aid schools. They could do so, but contributions did not count for grants. It was frequently economically preferable for an authority to keep going a school receiving a direct grant than to have full responsibility for it.

incremental salary scales, under the Burnham agreements, accentuated this development.

The cases in which governors are mentioned in Board of Education files concern endowed schools which did not fit into the pattern prescribed by regulations. In particular, the Board was disturbed when any question of continuing or reviving preparatory departments was raised, as such departments could not be grant-aided after 1922. Others referred to minor property changes over which governors had control.

In the main, such material as there is illustrates the operation of administrative procedures, and the function of the Board as regulator and referee. This presents a complete contrast with the stormy pre-war period when policy was determined between the Board, LEAs and governing bodies. The situation is well illustrated by the Leeds files of the period, which might be expected to provide a sequel to the battle between Morant and Graham. Among the mass of correspondence between the LEA and the Board, however, there is no reference to the activities of governing bodies, and it seems clear that this issue was regarded as settled for good. Clearly the governing bodies of endowed schools could be powerful and influential institutions during this period, particularly when their funds were appreciable; and some LEAs made it a cardinal principle to treat the governing bodies of maintained schools with similar respect.

There is little evidence of new thinking, save in the plans made by Henry Morris in Cambridgeshire for 'Village Colleges'.[34] His ultimate aim was to have, in about ten centres where senior elementary schools already existed, village colleges that would provide for the co-ordination and development of all forms of education—primary and secondary, further and adult (including agricultural)—together with social and recreational facilities, and at the same time furnish a community centre for the neighbourhood. He saw the control of these village colleges being vested in a body of governors responsible to the LEA and consisting of:

(a) The managing body of the senior elementary school. As the

[34] Morris, Henry, *The Village College*, Cambridge University Press, 1924.

school would serve more than one village, this body would be composed of managers appointed by the County Council, and others appointed by the minor local authorities of the areas served.

(b) Members appointed by the County Council as representing local interests, to supervise the higher education (including agricultural education) provided.

(c) A representative appointed by the Senate of the University of Cambridge.

(d) Representatives of other interests, e.g. the Parish Council as owners of the Recreation ground associated with each college.

Morris proposed that the governing body, when acting as a *whole*, should be advisory and consultative only (save in respect of higher and agricultural education). Executive acts in regard to other services would devolve on the constituent section statutorily responsible as, for example, in the case of the elementary school, on the managers. The governing body, in so far as it carried out services for which the County Council was the local authority, would be responsible to the County Council. Unfortunately there appears to be no material surviving to show what interest the Board took in Morris' proposals, although the latter formed in essence the pattern actually adopted by the county. His thinking is paralleled, however, in the Hadow Report on *The Education of the Adolescent* of 1926 (para. 199):

We think that a definite attempt might well be made to associate with the work of every Modern School and most, if not all, Senior Classes representative local men and women, who would be able to contribute knowledge and personal interest such as should be a constant help in developing the work of the school or class on lines suited to local needs and social conditions. The persons appointed to serve as managers should be representative in the widest sense, including members of different professions and persons concerned with commerce, industry, or agriculture, whether as employers or employees . . . It seems to us that a carefully chosen body of managers, including persons with special knowledge of local conditions and local peculiarities, might often be of great service to the Authority in matters connected with the conduct of the Modern School or Senior Class, more especially as forming a link between the staff, the parents of the pupils, and local employers. The managers might fulfil a very useful function, as indeed they often do at present, by explaining and interpreting to parents, local employers and the community generally the special province, function and aim of Modern Schools and Senior Classes.

The way was thus prepared for a more widespread adoption of managing and governing bodies throughout the school system. But the emphasis was not so much on their administrative role as upon the part they could play in interpreting the schools, and the publics they served, to each other. The marks of this new approach are to be seen in some aspects of the preparations leading up to the Education Act, 1944.

3 The Education Act, 1944 and the Role of the Department of Education and Science

THE PREPARATION OF THE 1944 ACT

The Education Act, 1944 introduced an educational system reconstituted in accordance with a major principle laid down in the Hadow Report: that there should be a clear distinction in terms of control, organization and accommodation between the primary and secondary stages of education. The Hadow proposals for the development of managing bodies for secondary modern schools are in line with, although they do not provide the ostensible or acknowledged source for, the Board of Education's first proposals for secondary school governing bodies. The first indication that the Board was indeed contemplating a system of individual bodies for all county secondary schools appeared in the White Paper of July 1943, *Educational Reconstruction*. But this made no reference to the possible development of managing bodies for primary schools. These were first mentioned in the subsequent draft Bill.

Paragraph 61 of the White Paper read:

It is desirable that any legislation should prescribe the status of the LEA in relation to all types of secondary schools, and that steps should be taken to give an authoritative definition of the status and powers of governing bodies. It is contemplated that every such school should have an Instrument of Government defining the constitution of its governing body, and the respective functions of governing bodies and the LEA. There is ample room for the exercise of powers by governors, particularly in the case of aided schools, over the general conduct of the school, including the appointment of teachers and the organisation and curriculum.

The section attracted little attention in the House of Commons debate on the White Paper held on 29 July 1943, the only reference to governing bodies being made by Mr Kenneth Lindsay (Independent, Kilmarnock), who thought there was a good case for seeing that the continuous life of the school was represented by a body of men who were not solely local councillors, but people of 'proved interest in education'.

In preparing the relevant section of the Education Bill, the Board of Education (as shown later in *Principles of Government in Maintained Secondary Schools*, Cmd. 6523/1944) had been in consultation with the local authority, teacher and other associations. These discussions resulted in five clauses, which survived unscathed.

The five clauses provided that every primary and secondary school, whether county or voluntary should have a body of managers or governors respectively; and that this body should be constituted according to an instrument of management or government drawn up by the authority. Further, there should be rules of management, drawn up by the authority, for primary schools; and, for secondary schools, articles of government determined by the local authority in the case of county schools and approved by the Minister in the case of voluntary schools. In controlled schools, whether primary or secondary, one-third of the managing or governing body were to be foundation members; in aided schools, the proportion was to be two-thirds. Provision was made for two or more schools to share a managing or governing body.

The five clauses were debated by the House of Commons on 9 March 1944, during the committee stage of the Bill, and a number of amendments were resisted. On Clause 16 (17 of the final Bill), Mr Jewson (Liberal-National, Great Yarmouth) moved that instruments of management should be approved by the Minister of Education, but this motion was withdrawn after Mr R. A. Butler had said that this would create an enormous burden for the Ministry. Two similar amendments requiring schemes of management and government to be in general conformity with Model Articles approved by the Minister were also withdrawn. There was a long and at times heated debate on an amendment which sought to reduce the proportion of foundation members on managing bodies. It was moved by Mr Clement Davies (Liberal, Montgomery) and attracted a considerable amount of backing from Welsh non-conformist MPs. It was pressed to a division, but was lost by 169 votes to 17.

In view of present day controversies, it is interesting to note that an attempt was made to secure a place for parents. Mr Harvey (Independent, Combined English Universities) moved that instruments should provide for at least one manager to be representative of parents. This was backed by a number of speakers, and no voices were heard in opposition to the principle of the motion although Captain Cobb (Conservative, Preston) pointed to the difficulty of recruiting parent representatives when there was no Parent-Teacher Association. In reply, Mr Chuter Ede said that the Government was in complete sympathy with the idea behind the amendment. He thought there would be difficulty over the machinery for selecting parent representatives, and that it should be left to the managers to see that at least one of their number was to be reckoned as representing parents. He hoped that note would be taken of the discussion in local education authority offices and by people responsible for the appointment of foundation managers. Mr Harvey then asked leave to withdraw his amendment as he thought that the view expressed by the Government would be of assistance in encouraging the appointment of managers representative of parents.

The Government successfully resisted other amendments that not less than one-third of the members of governing bodies should include parents and other persons who were not members of the local authority; and that a majority of persons appointed by the local authority should be appointed by the county district council for the area served by the school.

Section 18 empowered local education authorities to make arrangements for grouping schools. Mr Harvey moved another amendment to ensure that not more than four schools should be so grouped. He thought that were was a danger of local education authorities regarding administrative convenience as paramount.

In reply, Mr Butler said that he was unable to make legal provision to secure this, but it was not the intention of the Government to operate the clause so as to destroy the schools' independence. He would prefer not to set an upper limit, but to leave the clause as it was on the understanding that it would not be misused. He did not want to eliminate the power to amalgamate governing bodies, as he had been asked by the local authorities to keep this.

Throughout the debate left wing speakers were suspicious lest the prominence given to governing bodies by statute should mean the removal of publicly provided education from public control. Conservative opinion defended the position of the older schools. Kenneth Lindsay stoutly argued that there should be 'no handing over to local education authorities of secondary schools whose individuality had been handed down by successive headmasters'.

Middle or 'neutral' opinion supported the extension of the older pattern, so that the gap between major independent schools and publicly provided schools might be bridged. It was argued by Professor Gruffyd (Liberal, University of Wales) that county grammar schools could only compete with public schools if they had similar privileges and freedoms. Gruffyd's argument is the key to the understanding of the situation at the time of the passing of the Act. It was then by no means clear whether the older public schools and grammar schools could retain their varying degress of independence from the expanding state system. It was, therefore, expedient for their defenders to stress not their distinctiveness but the possibility of their most desirable features being more widely diffused.

GENERAL GUIDANCE TO LOCAL EDUCATION AUTHORITIES

There were, then, no amendments to the original clauses, and after the enactment of the Bill the Ministry issued the Command Paper to which reference has already been made. This set out in some detail the Ministry's philosophy of school government, and it was also stated that there was substantial agreement between the parties concerned. The Command Paper was intended to deal with those matters which bulked most largely in problems of school government and in regard to which the formulation of general provisions was most necessary. It pointed out that there are important differences between rural and urban areas, and between larger and smaller urban areas, and that it would be wise for local education authorities to consult minor authorities in their areas before framing articles. Every school was to have an individual life of its own as well as a place in the local system. The independence assured to aided schools made it all the more desirable to ensure that reasonable autonomy was enjoyed by county schools. Independence implied freedom to exercise legitimate and appropriate functions and Clause 17 recognized for the first time the need to define functions to be exercised by each of the parties involved. The pioneering nature of this section of the Bill had been recognized by a number of speakers in the debate on 9 March 1944 and was generally welcomed, although misgivings were expressed by Mr W. G. Cove. He felt that it would detract from the autonomy of local education authorities to set up governing bodies which might not contain elected members. Mr William Gallacher (Communist, West Fife) saw in the institution of governing bodies yet another outmoded form of class distinction.

In the Command Paper references were made to a number of matters, as follows: it was assumed that governing bodies would include adequate representation of the local education authority as well as provision for other people to serve whose qualifications enabled them to play a useful part in school government. A limited number of co-options was an advantage, and this practice might be continued. A proportion of women should be included on the boards of girls' and mixed schools. Among co-opted governors it would be appropriate to include university representatives and one or more persons associated with commercial and industrial life in the neighbourhood. There was general agreement that the interests of the teaching staff, parents, and old scholars should be reflected in the composition of the governing body. One of the bodies consulted thought that governors should be specially nominated for such purposes, but the others thought this unnecessary. No other guidance was given to local authorities as regards parental representation and it was left to them to decide how far and in what measure they should conform.

The Command Paper then discussed the functions to be exercised by governors. It was thought that in financial matters, 'The practice will no doubt generally obtain by which governors prepare estimates and submit them to the local education authority.' Within the broad headings of approved estimates governors should have latitude to exercise reasonable discretion. With regard to the appointment of heads, practices in local authority schools had varied very considerably in the past, and it was desirable that as far as possible there should be some greater uniformity. There had been a wide measure of agreement with associating governors and the local education authority at both stages, and two procedures were commended: under the first, the governors would consider the applicants with a representative of the authority present, and submit three names to a committee of the authority, a member of the governing body being present when the appointment was made. Under the second, which was said to be increasingly well-regarded, a joint committee would be set up, composed of a equal number of members of the governing body and of the authority. This committee, under the chairmanship of a member of the authority, would short-list and make the appointment.

For assistant staff the Command Paper advised that the usual practice should be for appointments to be made by the governors in consultation with the head, subject to confirmation by the authority. Vacancies should generally be notified in the first instance to the authority to avoid multiplicity of advertisements. The authority should be in a position to secure interchangeability, and appointment from a pool of junior staff. Dismissal of teaching staff could be made on the initiative either of the governing body or of the authority, although the final decision must rest with the latter. It was felt that the appointment of non-teaching staff should rest in practice with the governors, acting on the advice of the head and the authority, which should be in a position to require appointments to be made from a pool.

The division of functions in respect of internal organization and curriculum closely reflected the thinking of the nineteenth-century commissions. The local education authority was to have the right to frame both the development plan for the area, and subsequently to settle the general educational character of the school and its place in the local system. Subject to this general responsibility, the governors were to have general direction of the conduct and curriculum of the school. The head was to control the internal organization, management and discipline of the school, and was also to have the power to suspend pupils, subject to a report being made forthwith to the governors and the authority. It might be thought that this division of functions stood in need of elucidation, as there were possibilities of conflict between two or all three partners over their proposed responsibilities.

It was stressed that all proposals and reports affecting the conduct and curriculum of the school should be made available as long as possible beforehand. Decisions by the chairman of the governing body should be limited to urgent matters and reported without delay to the governors. The head should be entitled to attend throughout all meetings of the governing body, except as the latter might decide for good cause. Free consultation and co-operation should exist between the head and the chief education officer on matters affecting the welfare of the school, and suitable arrangements should be made for enabling the teaching staff to submit their proposals to the governing body through the head.

Whilst as far as possible the wishes of parents should be taken into account, it was for the local education authority to determine what type of education a child should receive. But governors and heads were to play an essential part in the selection of children for individual schools.

This Command Paper, together with the Model Articles which were subsequently issued for the guidance of local education authorities by the Ministry and which followed the recommendations of the Command Paper very closely, appeared to leave local authorities a good deal of scope. The articles of government were in every case to be approved by the Minister, and in particular they were to determine the functions to be exercised in relation to the school by the local education authority, the governors and the head. However, the Model Instrument of Government for county secondary schools left the local authority absolute discretion as to the number of governors and the manner of their appointment, since it spoke of a governing body as 'consisting of such a number of persons appointed in such a manner as the local education authority may determine.' As long as there was an Instrument and a group of persons who could be described as a body of governors, the Ministry would have few grounds for challenging the authority's proposals. Similarly, authorities appear to possess wide discretion in making arrangements for grouping two or more schools under one governing body: the only safeguard against wholesale grouping was Section 68 of the Education Act which stated that in the event of a local education authority acting unreasonably, the Minister might give a direction.

INSTRUMENTS AND ARTICLES OF GOVERNMENT

During the course of the research study a collection of instruments and articles of government was made, with the help of practically every local education authority. What follows is an analysis of their main features at the time of the enquiry. This analysis is set against the schedule containing a model instrument and model articles of government appended to the Administrative Memorandum No. 25 of 26 January 1945, already referred to.

INSTRUMENTS OF GOVERNMENT

Constitution of a Governing Body

There is no 'normal' size for a governing body, but a membership of twelve is usual. Members consist of *representative governors* appointed by the local education authority and other agencies, and *co-optative governors*, appointed by the governing body itself.

Representative Governors

Generally the *representative governors* do not have to be members of their appointing body, but in 7 county boroughs all the representative governors had to be members either of the Education Committee or of the Council, and in 4 small counties and in 12 county boroughs the number of representative governors who must be members either of the Education Committee or of the Council was specified. Other sources and categories from which representative governors were to be drawn were:

	Counties	County Boroughs and ILEA
Universities	17	6
Parents or PTAs	6	3
Industry and Commerce	3	6
Teaching Staff	2	I
'Persons of experience in education or acquainted with needs of area'	5	I
Religious bodies	2	–
Contributory Primary Schools	9	I
Persons with interest in immediate post-school period	3	I

Representation of *minor local authorities* was found in all counties except 7, up to a maximum of half of the membership of the governing body.

Provision for *ex-officio governors* was found in 21 county boroughs and 4 counties: in this category are found, for example, the mayor, the chairman and vice-chairman of the education committee or of the secondary education sub-committee and chairmen of local district councils. One county provides for its chief education officer to be an ex-officio member of all governing bodies.

Provision for *co-optative governors* was found in 36 counties (although 2 of these had such provision only in respect of grammar schools) and in 60 county boroughs; 6 counties and 9 county boroughs had co-optative governors. Generally speaking, no limitations were placed on the choice of co-optative governors. 24 counties and 29 county boroughs merely stated that they were appointed by the representative governors. There were some cases of specific sources being named, as the following table shows:

	Counties	County Boroughs
Universities	1	4
Parents or PTAs	1	8
Industry and Commerce	–	5
Teaching Staff	–	2
'Persons of experience in education or acquainted with the needs of the area'	4	7
Old Scholars	–	4
Representatives of Further Education	2	–

The fact that some authorities made no formal provision for the representation of specific interests does not necessarily mean that such interests are unrepresented; it will be seen later how governors ostensibly co-opted on an open basis are in fact recruited.

In some cases provision was made for *women members* as a separate category. In 18 counties and in 20 county boroughs it was stipulated that from 1 to 5 members of a governing body should be women.

Limitations in the Model Instrument on the *eligibility* of governors included the important provision that 'no master or other person employed for the purposes of the school shall be a governor'.

All but four counties followed the model. Two of these were even more restrictive, refusing to approve the appointment of anyone who worked for the County Council. The others made provision for teachers to be governors as follows:

(i) 'No teacher . . . except under such regulations as may be made in any particular case by the local education authority with regard to governors' representation of the teaching staff of the school'.

(ii) 'No teacher . . . shall be appointed as a governor, except where in the opinion of the Education Committee there are special circumstances, or except where such a teacher . . . being a member of the Borough, U.D. or Parish Council, is appointed a governor by such council'.

All but eight county boroughs followed the model. Of these 4 omitted the clause altogether, while 3 were more restrictive still, specifying that no person employed by the local education authority should be a governor. As it stands the model clause is ambiguous. It might be construed as a ban on teachers serving as governors of their own school, or of any school maintained by the authority. Some authorities have taken the former view, and have enforced a general prohibition simply by substituting 'schools' for 'school', the plural referring to the schools named in the Instrument. A further authority made the distinction more apparent by specifying that 'no teacher . . . shall be a governor of a school in which he holds an appointment'. The specific ban on teachers serving as governors does not preclude other people being appointed as teachers' representatives on governing bodies.

Appointment of Chairman

The model states that:

The governors shall at their first meeting in the year elect two of their number to be respectively the chairman and vice-chairman of their meetings for the year.

In the counties there were only two exceptions. In one the chairman and vice-chairman held office, unless otherwise determined, for the period coincident with the triennial period of office of the governors; and in the other the chairmanship was to be held by one of the representative governors appointed by the authority. This latter restriction was found in no fewer than 28 county boroughs. One authority was unique in that it did not allow the chairman or the vice-chairman to hold office for more than four consecutive years. Elsewhere they were eligible for re-election without qualification.

ARTICLES OF GOVERNMENT

It was stipulated in the 1944 Act (Section 17(3)(b)) that:

every county secondary school and every voluntary secondary school shall be conducted in accordance with articles of government . . . and such articles shall in particular determine the functions to be exercised in relation to the school by the local education authority, the body of governors, and the head teacher respectively.

The principal functions ascribed to governors are virtually the same in all the articles and relate to: finance, the appointment and dismissal of the head, assistant teachers and non-teaching staff, the general direction of the conduct and curriculum of the school, the care and use of school premises, school holidays, and the admission of pupils.

Finance

The functions of governors and authority are defined as follows:

(a) 'The governors shall in the month of . . . in each year submit for the consideration of the local education authority an estimate of the income and expenditure required for the purposes of the school for the 12 months ending . . . in the following year, in such a form as the local education authority may require.'

(b) 'The local education authority shall consider the estimate and make such variations in it as they think fit.'

(c) 'Where the governors are empowered by the local education authority to incur expenditure they shall not exceed the amount approved by the local education authority under each head of the estimates in any year without the previous consent of the local education authority.'

In 41 counties and 43 county boroughs articles followed the model, although in a number of cases authorities added their own explanatory clauses. Elsewhere the financial powers of governors were reduced. Only one authority went to the extreme of entirely omitting the financial clause from the articles, but in 8 other authorities governors were limited to making recommendations and proposals for special expenditures, and they were given no say in the preparation of estimates. Sub-section (c) above was missing from the articles of 13 county boroughs and some authorities included a clause to the general effect that governors were not to incur expenditure outside the estimates without the previous consent of the authority.

In 7 counties and 2 county boroughs only were governors allocated a sum of money which they could spend without reference to the authority. The maximum sum mentioned was £100; apart from another mention of £50, the remaining authorities set a limit of £25 or less. Even though such sums were sufficient only for odd repairs or minor improvements, these authorities felt that their governors appreciated this small token of financial independence. One authority, without giving their governors any special allowance, managed nonetheless to increase their concern with finance by allowing them to incur expenditures which were not provided for in the estimates, as long as they could save an equivalent amount under some other heading.

School funds, where they exist, are not normally the concern of governors, although if they are at all substantial they are usually subject to audit by the authority. However, in 7 counties and 7 county boroughs it was necessary for the governors to give their approval before fund money could be spent.

Appointment of Heads

The model articles provide for two alternative procedures:

Either 'The vacant post shall be advertised by the local education authority and a short-list of three names shall be drawn up from the applications for the post by the governors, a representative of the local education authority being present. The final appointment shall be made by the local education authority, a representative of the governors being present'.

Or 'The vacant post shall be advertised by the local education authority and a short-list shall be drawn up from the applications for the post by a Joint Committee consisting of an equal number of governors and representatives of the local education authority under the chairmanship of a person nominated by the local education authority. The said Joint Committee shall also meet to interview the persons on the short-list, and shall recommend one person on the list for appointment by the local education authority.'

The first method is not found in any of the counties and in only 16 county boroughs. Some chief education officers consider that it is not popular with governors because, although they may recommend three candidates, there is no guarantee that the authority will not bring in someone else, or that the least favoured of the three will not be appointed. The second method, which gives the governors a far more definite role, is followed by 26 counties and 21 county boroughs. On the whole those authorities which follow neither of these alternatives tend to give their governing bodies more responsibility rather than less. In 14 county boroughs, when the authority has advertised and received the applications, they hand the short-listing and interviewing over to the governors, who are then simply required to submit one name to the authority for confirmation. This practice is also followed in 3 counties. In a very few cases, authorities merely retain the right to veto any candidate recommended by the governors. In 6 county boroughs and 3 counties the authority's participation is more positive in that they prepare a short-list and then leave it to their governing bodies to interview and select a candidate. Sometimes a representative of the authority is present during the two latter stages.

Those authorities which delegate a large part of the responsibility for the appointment of heads to their governors do so on the argument that if the latter are to have real responsibility for their school it is essential that they should be involved in the appointment of the head. Since governors know their school—in theory—better than any other group of outsiders, and since the success of a school depends very much on the head and on his relationships with the staff, it is the governors who are best qualified to judge the suitability of a man for the headship of a particular school. Not all authorities accept this argument. Their case for minimizing the part played by governors is that in the first place the governors know their school too well to be objective about the sort of leadership it may need, and that they are likely to favour local candidates unreasonably; and secondly, that they cannot have regular experience of selecting senior staff. One simple way in which authorities can reduce governors' participation is by weighting the Joint Committee in their own favour. To judge by the experience of one authority where this is done, governors taking part in appointment meetings lose interest, as the authority does not need to take their views into account.

In considering the methods used in the appointment of heads in the county boroughs, it is necessary to bear in mind the different ways in which even standard articles can be interpreted. These may appear to give governors substantial powers, but this can mean little, if the governing body is virtually no more than a subcommittee of the education committee. This matter will be dealt with in more detail in the section of this report concerned with governing bodies for large groups of schools. (p. 69)

Appointment of Assistant Masters and Non-Teaching Staff

The Model Articles, in dealing with the appointment of teaching and non-teaching staff, offer local education authorities the utmost flexibility. Authorities, if they think fit, may advertise a post, but they need not do so; they may require the governors to fill a post with a master transferred from another school, or from any pool of new entrants to the teaching profession. Apart from slight variations in the wording, all but 6 of the county boroughs follow section 6(a) and (b) of the Model Articles, which reads:

(a) 'On the occurrence of a vacancy for an assistant master the Governors shall notify the local education authority who shall, if they think fit, advertise the post and shall transmit to the Governors the names of the candidates. Provided that the local education authority may, if they think fit, and after having given full consideration to the views of the Governors and the Headmaster, require the Governors to appoint a new master to be transferred from another school or from any pool of new entrants to the teaching profession.'

(b) 'The appointment of assistant masters shall be made to the service of the local education authority by the Governors in consultation with the Headmaster within the limits of the establishment of staff laid down for the current year by the local education authority, and such appointments shall, except when made under the proviso to paragraph (a) of this Article, be subject to confirmation by the local education authority.'

In 3 authorities the short-list is drawn up by the headmaster and the chief education officer; in two the authority makes the appointment through its staffing sub-committee, and in one there is no mention of who actually makes the appointment. In 4 counties the articles deviate from the model as follows:

(1) The governors are to notify the authority of vacancies, and to state what qualifications candidates should possess.

(2) Appointments are to be made by a joint committee of the education committee and the governors.

(3) The short-list is to be drawn up by the head in consultation with the chairman of governors and a sub-committee of the governors which is formed for this specific purpose; the candidates are then to be interviewed by the governors.

(4) Appointments are to be made by the headmaster.

The model article states that the appointments of assistant teaching staff shall in all cases be determinable upon x months' notice in writing. Generally the amount of notice which an assistant teacher is required to give is two months, but in many of the articles this is increased to three months in the summer term. Whereas there is a great deal of flexibility as to the appointment of assistant teachers, the procedure for the dismissal of both heads and assistants is laid down with uniform precision, and all the articles have essentially followed the standard model.

As regards non-teaching staff the model article provides that governors should appoint to the service of the authority after consultation with the headmaster. Dismissal is by the authority on the recommendation of the governors. In 46 county boroughs and 29 counties this clause was adopted in essence. In 24 county boroughs the appointments were left entirely in the hands of the authority, and in the others a distinction was made between the different types of non-teaching staff, with the governors appointing some, usually the caretakers and groundsmen, and the authorities appointing the rest. In 4 counties the authority was solely responsible for the appointment and dismissal of non-teaching staff, and in 5 responsibility for appointments was shared by authorities and governors.

Organization and Curriculum

The section in the model articles dealing with organization and curriculum is divided into three parts. The first two are as follows:

(a) 'The local education authority shall determine the general educational character of the school and its place in the local educational system. Subject thereto the governors shall have the general direction of the conduct and curriculum of the school.'

(b) 'Subject to the provisions of these Articles the Headmaster shall control the internal organization, management and discipline of the school, shall exercise supervision over the teaching and non-teaching staff, and shall have the power of suspending pupils from attendance for any cause which he considers adequate, but on suspending any pupil he shall forthwith report the case to the governors, who shall consult the local education authority.'

24 counties and 64 boroughs substantially followed the above wording.

Variations can be classified as follows:

(1) Authorities in which the head's responsibility is given in more detail: '. . . the Head shall be responsible for the choice of books, the method of teaching, the arrangement of classes, and the time-table . . .'

This variation is found in 3 counties and 1 county borough, with one county adding that 'the Head shall determine subject to the governors' approval in what proportion any aggregate sum approved by the authority for expenditure upon school plant and apparatus and prizes shall be appropriated to specific purposes', and the county borough adding the words 'and generally the whole internal organization, management and discipline of the school'.

(2) Authorities in which the 'general direction of the conduct and curriculum of the school' is

(a) shared by the governors with the head (4 counties, 4 county boroughs)

(b) exercised by the governors subject to the general direction of the local education authority, or else transferred to the local education authority (4 counties, 2 county boroughs)

(c) exercised by the governors, but restricted to the 'conduct of the school and the welfare of the children' (1 county)

(d) exercised by the head, subject to the governors' approval (1 county)

(e) not referred to at all (3 county boroughs)

(3) Authorities modifying the provision for the suspension of pupils

(a) In 5 counties the authority is not only consulted by the governors, but has to be informed by the head at the same time as he informs his governors

(b) In 5 counties and 2 county boroughs suspension by the headmaster follows prior consultation with the chairman of governors or there is stated provision for parental appeal.

The third part of the section on organization and curriculum lays down prescriptions for communications between the various parties concerned with school government:

(c) (i) 'There shall be full consultation at all times between the Headmaster and the Chairman of Governors.

(ii) All proposals and reports affecting the conduct and curriculum of the school shall be submitted formally to the Governors. (The Chief Education Officer or his representative shall be informed of such reports and proposals and shall be furnished with a copy thereof at least seven days before they are considered.)

(iii) The Headmaster shall be entitled to attend throughout every meeting of the Governors, except on such occasion and for such times as the Governors may for good cause otherwise determine.

(iv) There shall be full consultation and co-operation between the Headmaster and the Chief Education Officer on matters affecting the welfare of the school.

(v) Suitable arrangements shall be made for enabling the teaching staff to submit their views or proposals to the Governors through the Headmaster.'

In their insistence that the head should have direct access to the chairman of governors and that there should be full consultation between the head and the chief education officer these clauses are reminiscent of the struggles of the Morant era. The strength accorded to the head's position is further reflected in the provision for him to attend meetings of the governors. In only one county borough did he have to be invited to attend his governors' meetings, but in all the rest he attended as of right. Similarly, only one county did not expressly state that the head was entitled to attend meetings, and even here he was to have full opportunity to consult with the governors and to express his views on matters coming within his province.

Variations in the wording of clause (v) are found in 10 counties and 5 county boroughs. In 4 county boroughs and 1 county the staff have the right to send a deputation to the governors' meetings, and in 1 county two governors are nominated by the governing body for the purpose of receiving deputations from the staff. In three cases the staff may submit a written report to the governors; finally in 4 counties the staff are entitled to make direct representations to the governors through the clerk. In all the head is to be informed in advance of the views and proposals which the teaching staff wish to submit.

The Care and Use of School Premises

The clause in the model articles has two parts:

(a) 'The governors shall from time to time inspect, and keep the local education authority informed as to the condition and state of repair of the school premises, and where the local education authority so permit, the governors shall have the power to carry out urgent repairs up to such an amount as may be approved by the local eduation authority.'

(b) 'The governors shall, subject to any direction of the local education authority, determine the use to which the school premises, or any part thereof, may be put out of school hours.'

Reference to urgent repairs was omitted by just under half of the county boroughs (35), but by only 3 counties. Among the counties 5 indicated the amount which the governors were not to exceed—this varied from £10 to £50.

Part (b) of the clause was not to be found in the articles of 6 county boroughs, and in a further 3 it was the authority which determined the use of the school premises. The counties which differed from the model fall into two groups: those which gave instructions as to payment for the letting of the premises, and those which expanded the original clause by giving more specific details.

School Holidays

The model articles give the governors the power to 'grant mid-term or other occasional holidays not exceeding ten days in any year'. The articles of 59 county boroughs either quoted the model exactly, or replaced it in part by the phrase '. . . not exceeding in any year the number of days approved by the local education authority.' In the remaining authorities the number of days which the governors could declare holidays was less than ten, and in some cases they were limited to a fixed number of half-days. The 13 county authorities which did not follow the model either reduced the number of days which the governors could grant or substituted a quota of half-days.

Admission of Pupils

The model states that the admission of pupils is to be in accordance with the arrangements made by the local education authority, but attention is to be paid to school records, the wishes of parents, and the views of the headmaster and the governors.

All county boroughs have adopted the model, save for one

which omits mention of parental choice. In 5 county authorities it is stressed that 'admission of pupils is to be in accordance with the regulations of the local education authority'.

Clerk to the Governors

In county schools it is usual for the chief education officer or his representative to be clerk to the governors. The clause specifying the appointment of a clerk is to be found either in the Articles—normally in the section dealing with the appointment of non-teaching staff—or in the Instrument. The model clause runs as follows: 'The Clerk of the Governors shall be the Chief Education Officer or such other person as may be appointed by the local education authority.'

In only 2 county boroughs is the model not followed. In one, provision is made for the town clerk to be clerk, but the chief education officer or his representative may attend meetings; in the other the clerk is to be the chief education officer, but the governors are to appoint their own correspondent.

In 25 counties the model applies, and in a further 12 the second part of the clause is omitted, so that it reads 'The Clerk to the Governors will be the Chief Education Officer'.

In 5 counties the governors can recommend to the authority the person whom they wish to have appointed. However, in practice in all but 7 county authorities the clerk is either the chief education officer or someone 'from the office'. The 7 authorities which practise local clerking do so for one of two reasons: either because they think that it is impossible for a small authority to take on the clerking of all managing and governing bodies; or because they think that governing bodies should have the degree of independence which local clerking might give them.

TWO DISPUTED DRAFT SCHEMES OF GOVERNMENT

Some time has been spent on the detailed examination of instruments and articles because, although in the day to day administration of a school they may seem to have little relevance, they are of importance in defining the overall pattern of educational administration. Certainly this is suggested by the care with which the Ministry surveys and comments upon articles of government, which local education authorities must submit for approval. This is not simply because of a concern with governing bodies as such, and as means by which substance can be given to the concept of the school as an institution possessing a measure of individuality and independence. This concern is real enough. But there are two other purposes which are reflected in the attitude taken by the Ministry in cases where a stand is felt to be necessary. One is that the provisions of the education acts must be complied with; the other is that it is essential to safeguard an accepted and generally understood pattern of administrative relationships. Instruments and articles are important because they define the respective roles of heads and local education authorities; because they ascribe responsibilities for the appointment and dismissal of teaching and non-teaching staff; and because they are a means by which the Ministry can from time to time concern itself with the administration of schools provided both by local authorities and voluntary bodies alike. Two cases may serve to show how the Ministry reacted to local education authorities who delayed in submitting schemes or whose schemes were considered unsatisfactory.

One county borough submitted its draft articles in July 1948, some three and a half years after Administrative Memorandum No. 25 had been issued. They contained a clause to the effect that assistant teaching staff should be appointed by the appointments sub-committee of the local education authority. The Ministry thought this unsatisfactory, and that the authority should follow the model articles, which stated that assistant masters should be appointed to the service of the authority by the governors in consultation with the head. The chief education officer replied that his authority refused to alter the clause, and nothing more happened for two years. In July 1950 the Ministry pointed out that the clause provided for the authority to advertise posts and transmit the names of candidates to the governors, but did not indicate who was to appoint assistant masters, or deal with applications. The chief education officer replied in a semi-official letter in the following month, asking the Ministry to send an official letter of objection to the proposed clause if it wished him to refer the matter officially to his committee. Almost by return the Ministry wrote to say that its letter of the previous month still stood, and that it awaited further action. In April 1951 it sent a reminder and two months later received a reply stating that the authority preferred its own clause. The Ministry replied officially to this in the following November, saying that this state of affairs was unsatisfactory, and that the draft Articles would be incomplete without the inclusion of the clause in the form suggested. The authority did not reply until April 1953, when the chief education officer stated that his authority could see no advantage in the alteration proposed. After five years of fruitless negotiation, the Ministry concluded that deadlock had been reached. The authority was regarded as obtuse and obstructive, and other approaches were canvassed. That of asking the Association of Education Committees to intervene was not thought desirable at this stage. It is not clear what were the objections to doing this; but it may have been felt that a united front might develop against ministerial pressure. Action under Section 68 of the 1944 was considered. This could apparently be done on the grounds that the authority had delayed unduly in fulfilling its statutory duty to submit a satisfactory scheme and in refusing to facilitate ministerial approval of the articles. In an earlier leading case, the Ministry had been advised that it could review a decision by an authority in the light of Section 68 only if the decision contained an element of perversity, and could not be justified on a fair balance of the circumstances. In the event, the matter seemed to the Ministry to be one in which Section 68 could be invoked, and it was proposed that a final warning should be sent before a directive was issued. There was no scope for further personal approaches to the chief education officer, and it was decided to write officially to the authority, asking that the reconsideration of the articles should be treated as urgent. A letter to this effect was sent in June 1953 and the Ministry wrote yet again in January 1954 to find out whether it had been put before the committee in proper form. At the same time it was suggested that the District Inspector should take the opportunity of raising the matter on his next visit to the authority; he could hint that the Ministry would be very much on the warpath unless the authority agreed to comply. The District Inspector's intervention quickly produced results. He wrote to the chief education officer at the beginning of February 1954, saying that he would be making an informal approach to secure the authority's agreement, and six weeks afterwards the authority agreed to a revision of the clause acceptable to the Ministry.

It is not immediately apparent why the Ministry refused to stomach the offending clause and thought that it formed an appropriate issue for intervention under Section 68. It must, however, be conceded that on the basis of the evidence available, the authority simply dug its toes in and did not give any reasoned case for preferring its own clause. The Ministry had stronger grounds for invoking Section 68 by virtue of the authority's failure to submit a scheme of any sort after a very protracted period. However, this was not regarded as the main point at issue, and since the model articles were described as 'suggestions' there would appear to be grounds for local education authorities to consider even substantial modifications within, of course, the limits imposed by the education acts themselves.

Another example repays study. By September 1949 no scheme of government had been received from one authority, and the Ministry wrote officially to express concern, in the following gently ironic terms:

The Minister appreciates that the preparation of Articles may present some difficulty, but feels that it should have been possible to overcome these in the four years since Administrative Memorandum No. 25 was issued.

This was followed up in January 1950 by a personal letter to the chief education officer in which it was stated that the Ministry was now very much concerned: in the past two years four official letters had been sent to which no replies had been received. What was holding matters up? A week later the chief education officer replied that he had only just taken up his post, and he would see what could be done when the pressure on him had relaxed. The Ministry then decided to send regular reminders to the authority and wrote again in April expressing still more concern that no proposals for setting governing bodies had been received. It requested that a draft be submitted for approval without delay. This letter was followed by a reminder in July, to which the chief education officer replied that he hoped to submit a scheme by the autumn. In January 1951 he wrote to the effect that the authority wanted a single governing body for all its secondary schools, and wished to know if the Ministry had any objections. The opinion of the District Inspector, who was now drawn in, was that this was a most disappointing reaction, as it was quite impossible for any single governing body to take the leisurely and personal interest in each of several schools that had been characteristic of the best grammar school governing bodies. If grouping were to be adopted, the Ministry should suggest a nucleus of governors to serve each school, but it was doubtful whether it could compel the authority to modify its proposal. In March the Ministry replied officially to the effect that if too many schools were grouped together, the administrative gain might be outweighed by loss in other respects, as it was difficult to see how one governing body could reflect the interests of a large number of schools, each with an individual life of its own. It suggested that the authority might like to consider additions of one or two members for each school or type of school, these members attending only when their own schools were being discussed. The governing body should be specially constituted, and should not be a sub-committee of the authority.

In June 1951 the Ministry asked what progress was being made, and the chief education officer replied that he hoped to submit draft articles in September. This was done, but the following month the Ministry asked the authority to review a number of the provisions they contained. These included clauses laying down that the proceedings of governing bodies should be submitted to the education committee for confirmation; that the appointment of teaching staff should be made subject to the orders, rules and regulations of the education committee (the Ministry thought that these appointments should be subject to written agreement and that it was also desirable that procedure for dismissals should be set out in the articles); and that the head teachers should attend meetings of the governing body upon the invitation of the governors (the Ministry held that they should be entitled to attend meetings at which their schools were being discussed). The Ministry sent reminders in January and March 1952 and the chief education officer submitted revised articles in May, which caused the Ministry to ask for reconsideration of a clause running: 'The Education committee shall normally advertise a vacancy for a Head Teacher, having decided whether this should be filled by limited or open competition.' The chief education officer had mentioned that it was established practice to fill headships by transfer or promotion, but the Ministry did not agree to this, and thought that 'normally' should be deleted. The chief education officer also said that the attendance of heads at governors' meetings by invitation was regarded as the only practical method when there was only one governing body. The teachers' associations in the authority had been consulted and had raised no objections.

In considering these latest developments, the Ministry did not think it worthwhile challenging the authority on its appointments system. It was allowed to have its way under protest. With regard to the attendance of heads, it was clear that the governing body would be rarely concerned with the affairs of individual schools and would act indistinguishably from a sub-committee. The Ministry came to the conclusion that there was no way of preventing this, although it was quite against the spirit of the 1944 Act. The trouble was that the authority did not regard governing bodies as necessary or desirable, and had no intention of letting its customary practices be obstructed.

In both of the cases considered there is an interesting difference in the tone of the official and unofficial letters that passed between the Ministry and the authority, and in both cases also the District

Inspector played a significant part. For example, in the second case, it was to the Inspector that the chief education officer explained that when he first took up his appointment he was determined not to have individual governing bodies: from his previous experience he knew it was very difficult to stop councillors visiting schools too frequently and interfering in their management. He was determined to protect the schools in his new authority and was quite prepared to battle with the Ministry by the simple expedient of sitting on official letters.

Apart from the drastic step of invoking the powers of direction conferred in Section 68, there seems to be no effective means available to the Ministry to ensure the adoption of any model articles against determined opposition. One can only speculate what might have happened if the first authority discussed had not listened to the District Inspector. The Ministry undoubtedly followed a consistent policy of persuading authorities to keep to the spirit of the Command Paper recommendations and not to seek to reduce governing bodies to the status of minor executive agencies. But it does not seem to have recognized the role which it could have played if it had made authorities aware of practices adopted elsewhere and seems to have made no attempt to break down the isolation characteristic, in particular, of some county boroughs.

THE CONSIDERATION OF AMENDMENTS

Material is available from a number of authorities which throws light on the part played by the central authority in the amendment of schemes of government.

In one county borough the chief education officer was disturbed when a governing body concerned with several schools set up a sub-group of its members to deal with the staffing at the grammar school separately. He decided it was essential to secure a revision of the articles and wrote informally to the Department in April 1965. He did not refer to the situation which had developed, but pointed out that the education committee would, with the progress of secondary reorganization, need to take firmer control of the appointment of teaching staff. He asked for the Department's likely reaction to the insertion of a clause permitting the authority to waive the usual appointments procedure when necessary, to 'avoid redundancies and to make the best use of the available teaching man-power.'

Inside the Department it was considered that, as the articles were based on the agreed model, the proposed changes raised potentially important policy issues. They might, in fact, have unforeseen consequences for teacher-authority relations. The Department therefore replied in July that until secondary reorganization had settled down it would be reasonable for the authority, as an interim measure, to exercise firm control.

In another authority a proposal was put forward, in 1958, to set up several governing bodies to replace the existing single governing body for all secondary schools. Appointments of teaching staff, however, were to be made by the authority. In its reply in the following month the Ministry asked why teaching staff should not be appointed by the governors in accordance with the terms of the model articles. This produced an unofficial and very full letter from the chief education officer in which the implications of the local situation were presented. In an authority like his own it was better to appoint teaching staff to a pool than to a particular school. Often the authority had no specific vacancy in mind, and, indeed, specific vacancies could not always be forecast. Schools would rarely be staffed unless steps were taken long in advance, and governors could not act save when there was a known post to be filled. There had been long delays in the replacement of specialist staff. The head concerned was always consulted, and in practice appointments would always be made by the chief education officer and the head, and reported later to the committee. The chief education officer believed that in matters of promotion it was not always easy for inexperienced laymen to drive out personal considerations. The appointment of administrative staff was a function transferred to senior officers some time before, and the chief education officer wished to extend this practice to cover teaching staff, who knew that they would have a fair deal from him. It was a real achievement for the elected members to have succeeded in arriving at agreement to delegate powers to appoint to trusted officers. If the official view was that governors should be directly responsible for appointments, the sentiment it represented was admirable, but the chief education officer wished that those who advised the Minister had had some practice in the actual job.

The District Inspector found these arguments not unpersuasive as the system proposed had the merits of efficiency and justice; with regard to the former, speed was crucial, and anticipation of future needs wise. It also allowed for staff to be redeployed as necessary. There were, it was true, occasionally grounds for thinking that appointments by governing bodies were influenced by personal considerations; similarly, there might be reasons for thinking that one or two chief education officers (though certainly not this one) might, even though trusted by their committee, be guilty of partiality and petty tyranny.

In its reply the Ministry argued that the governors' interest might be increased if they had a say in the appointment of teaching staff. This produced an official letter from the chief education officer which he hoped would be read in the light of his earlier unofficial correspondence. He now argued that the appointment of assistants was a comparatively routine matter, and that he was not thinking of taking out of the hands of the governors the award of special responsibility or head of department posts. He would also like the governors to be allocated a block sum for general use. Spending power would make governors feel that they were really doing an independent job, but it was difficult to take any such power out of the hands of a rate-raising authority. The system constituted an experiment which could be reviewed in a year or two, and the authority had in mind further changes which would give governors even more financial control.

In the light of this very full statement by the chief education officer of the situation in this authority, the Ministry found it easy to approve the revised scheme. Although it was not feasible to require any periodical review, the District Inspector might suggest the articles should be reviewed when he thought the time was ripe.

Some three years later the same county sought approval for a procedure by which short-listing for headships should be done by the authority. Appointment would rest with the governors, subject to the approval of the authority. The Ministry noted that this would be a reversal of the model articles, but that it enabled the governors to play a greater part in the appointment of heads while still giving the authority the final word. In an unofficial letter it was suggested to the chief education officer that the governors should have an observer at the short-listing stage to see fair play. The chief education officer replied that short-listing was very fairly conducted by the chairman and deputy chairman of the education committee and himself. Before, when he had had his suspicions about favouritism, he had done the short-listing himself. The governors were also involved, in that some of them were members of the education committee, which would give formal approval to the short-list. Six months later, and without further comment, the proposal was approved by the Ministry.

These two cases illustrate the extent to which chief education officers can, through both official and unofficial correspondence, influence Civil Service attitudes in matters in which they have committee support. Indeed, in the first the entire initiative for revising the articles came from the chief education officer, who thought that it was not sufficient to follow the practice of many of his colleagues and let them lie forgotten. He felt that if they were to be taken seriously and literally they could lead to all sorts of difficulties. For its own part, the Department leaned heavily on the advice of the District Inspector, and the wish of the second chief education officer that ministerial advisers should have had some experience of doing the actual job is not without point. It was apparently left to the District Inspector to point out that there were authorities which suffered from acute shortage of staff, and that the standard procedure for involving governors in the making of appointments was more likely to leave the school un-staffed than to give the governors a worthwhile job. Nor was it apparently appreciated that, although the articles were static, the educational system was dynamic, and that the delineation of functions which might have been considered appropriate in 1944 might not be wholly applicable at a time when secondary re-organization was proceeding apace, and when other changes were occurring.

In these, as in other cases brought to light, the Ministry, and later the Department, does not seem to be concerned with the realities of educational administration as these present themselves to the authorities. Its concern with the drafting of clauses in articles of government seems to be out of all proportion, especially when it is considered that there exists no effective way of requiring authorities to devise and operate a live and vigorous system of school government. Apart from the very serious step of invoking Section 68 of the 1944 Act, there were no obvious sanctions which the Department could use. The most it could do was to enlist the influence of District Inspectors with recalcitrant chief education officers, and in some cases this strategy seems to have been successful.

To understand the central authority's attitude and its reactions in specific instances it is necessary to appreciate the several purposes served by section 68 of the Education Act, 1944, the Command Paper of 1943 and the Model Articles of 1945.

In the first place these provide a legal framework which the Minister must ensure is formally complied with and, if necessary, interpret. In the second place they define, in very considerable detail, the agreed working relationships of the central authority, local education authorities and governing bodies; and they also prescribe the place to be accorded to heads and teachers in the administrative setting. Finally, they incorporate a 'philosophy' of school government, the historical development of which has already been traced, and which ascribes value to a body of informed men and women being associated with individual schools.

In respect of the legal framework, and its formal expression, the Minister is on firm ground, since its primacy, save as a final arbiter, is assured. In respect of the definition of the respective responsibilities of the agencies involved its role is difficult, since there is wide room for differences of interpretation of rights and duties, and the practical outcome of any dispute depends on the relative strengths and bargaining power of teachers associations, local political parties, lay pressure groups, and even the determination and persuasiveness of individual men and women. The third area identified, the 'philosophy' of school government, is nebulous, but within it there are certain dominant ideas concerning the role of the head and school-community relationships which have proved to be remarkably persistent. Here, Board, Ministry and Department have in turn patiently reiterated the arguments in favour of schools having governing bodies. But they have been faced by education committees, administrative officers, heads and teachers often with substantial reasons for throwing doubt on them. Some, though not all, of the seeming inconsistencies of official policy and action in the instances cited, both in the early years of the century and more recently, may be explained in the light of this analysis.

There is, for example, the Enfield Grammar School case in 1967. The local education authority, in a scheme for reorganizing secondary education, planned to turn this selective (and voluntary controlled) school into a non-selective school. This aroused a group of objectors to seek a declaration in the High Court that the authority was contravening the school's articles of government, clause 11 of which read:

The arrangements for the admission of pupils to the school shall be such as may be agreed between the Governors and the Local Education Authority, and shall take into account the wishes of the parents, any school records and any other information which may be available, the general type of education most suitable for the particular pupil and the views of the Headmaster as to the admission of the pupil to the school, provided that the Local Education Authority shall determine which candidates are qualified for admission by reason of their having attained a sufficient educational standard.

It was also claimed that the local education authority had not acted in accordance with article 9:

. . . the Local Education Authority shall determine the general educational character of the school and its place in the local educational system, and subject thereto the Governors shall in consultation with the Headmaster be responsible for the general direction of the conduct and curriculum of the school.

The objection was that the authority had been able to determine the 'character' and 'place' of the school when the articles were first agreed, but that the decision, once taken, could not subsequently be modified.

The objectors won their case, the judgement being that article 11 clearly provided for the school to be selective and that its proposed non-selective character contravened article 9. Since the words 'from time to time' did not form part of this article the authority had no powers to alter in any way what had already been decided and approved. It was therefore necessary for the authority to seek approval from the Department for a reconstitution of the school (as provided for in section 13 of the Education Act, 1944) and for re-drafted articles.

At this point another difficulty arose. When articles are revised a reasonable time must be allowed for objections to be made. In his haste to help an authority of like political complexion, the then Secretary of State for Education (Mr Patrick Gordon Walker) allowed only four days for such objections to be made. An injunction was sought, and a stay of 28 days granted. At the end of this period, the articles were duly approved and the authority's plans could go forward.

The judgement can be criticized as excessively narrow on several counts. No account was apparently taken of the relative priority of the various articles nor was it appreciated that article 11 could be construed sensibly only in relation to article 9. Moreover the reference to 'the determination of the general educational character of the school' was not interpreted in relation to the very next words in the same article, namely the determination of the place of the individual school in the local educational system. Indeed it does not seem to have been appreciated that the powers mentioned in the articles derive from the general duty of the local education authority to provide a full and sufficient range of schools catering for pupils of all ranges of age, ability and aptitude. Articles of government are only one of a number of relevant provisions in the 1944 Act, and it is difficult to substantiate the claim that the articles are the ultimate bedrock on which a local authority's control of the school rests. Attention was concentrated almost exclusively on the formal provisions with virtually no account being taken of the actual relationship between the governing body and the local education authority—a matter of some importance in respect of county as well as voluntary schools.

However, the judgement stands or falls on Mr Justice Donaldson's construction of Article 9, and his view, confessedly not an authoritative statement, that the articles do not permit the local education authority to alter its determination of the general educational character of the school in the absence of the words 'from time to time' and that such determination must then be a once for all operation. This view is in flat contradiction to the relevant section of the Interpretation Act of 1889 (clause 32) (i) which reads as follows:

Where an Act passed after the commencement of this Act confers a power or imposes a duty, then unless the contrary intention appears, the power may be exercised and the duty shall be performed from time to time as occasion requires.

No mention was made of this clause during the case, and this omission has struck several observers as nothing short of astonishing. One possible explanation may lie in the extreme haste with which the entire case was conducted.[1]

What happened at Enfield illustrates the ever-present difficulty in a time of rapid change of reconciling that which is required by law with the need to plan and re-shape social institutions. As one commentator pointed out:

. . . if the very precise requirements of the statute had to be complied

---

[1] These aspects of the Enfield Grammar School case are not discussed by R. J. Buxton in his otherwise full review in—*Local Government* (*1970*), pp. 209-10.

with, and if working to legal rule was accepted as the overriding principle, then the education service might well grind to a halt and the object of the law be forfeited.[2]

But it must also be realized that schemes of government of all kinds exist to ensure that institutions should serve the purposes for which they are intended. This was the essence of the reforms of the nineteenth century and the reason which led the Board of Education to seek, through the issue of regulations and model articles, to ensure that the character of both old and new schools should be preserved and not destroyed or distorted by local authorities and their officers.

[2] *Times Educational Supplement*, 1 September 1967, p. 353.

4 Local Education Authorities and Governing Bodies

It has been seen that articles of government of county secondary schools are scrutinized carefully by the Department. Instruments, however, and hence the structure and membership of governing bodies are matters which are the concern of local authorities. Indeed, it cannot be otherwise, if they are to have effective control of their schools. The latent powers that reside in articles, and which were exemplified in the Enfield case, make it important to elected representatives and officers alike that they should develop structures of school management and government which will not get out of control. Even where it is argued that governing bodies have little significance there is reluctance to accept as members parents, teachers and others who are not vouched for by political parties or by institutions or individuals acceptable to councillors and officers. To the latter in particular, *predictability* in the behaviour of the individuals and groups with which they work is essential.

One simple and obvious way of exercising control, and one which is economical of administrative time, is that of limiting the number of people actually required to serve as managers or governors. This can be done by reducing the number of managing or governing bodies and grouping two or more schools together for governing purposes. Local education authorities follow a variety of grouping practices which reflect fundamentally different attitudes to governing bodies.

THE COUNTY BOROUGHS AND GROUPING

The differences in county boroughs are particularly striking, but the following classification is possible:

Category A County boroughs with individual governing bodies   21
Category B County boroughs with small groups (2 or 3 schools) 25
Category C County boroughs with large groups (4 or more
            schools)   12
Category D County boroughs with one governing body for all
            schools   20
                                                                ——
            Total   78

14 authorities in category B and 1 in category C had either individual governing bodies or separate groups for selective schools; 2, both in category B, had separate governing bodies for boys' schools and girls' schools; in the remainder, schools were grouped by area.

Size of authority, political complexion and the incidence of voluntary schools are factors that might seem likely to influence the pattern of government of county secondary schools. But it is certainly difficult to draw any firm conclusions as to the influence of size, as the following table shows:

Population	A	B	C	D	Total
200,000	3	2	5	7	17
100,000 and under 200,000	8	9	6	5	28
70,000 and under 100,000	5	7	1	7	20
Under 70,000	5	7	-	1	13
	21	25	12	20	78

Although it is true that in general the larger the authority, the more likely it is to be found in categories C or D, the exceptions are sufficient in number to reject size as a determining factor. For example, categories A and B include authorities with populations of over 200,000, while 8 authorities with less than 100,000 are found in group D. The purest group is C, 11 of whose members have a population of 100,000 or more.

A more definite pattern of control emerges from a consideration of political party control, as it was in 1967, at the time of the field studies. It can be argued that, at that point, the distribution of control was substantially typical of the post-war period. Omitting

3 authorities where the parties had equal representation, half the Labour authorities, or 25 out of 50, were in groups C or D, as opposed to a quarter, or 6 out of 25, of the Conservative boroughs. The boroughs where political control was marginal in 1966 divided equally between the two main parties and thus do not distort the main totals. The differences are particularly striking in authorities with a population of under 200,000, where the bias in favour of large groups or one governing body for all schools is not apparent. In this category 17 Labour-controlled authorities out of 38, but only 3 of 21 Conservative authorities, are found in groups C and D. It appears therefore that Labour-controlled authorities tend not to have governing bodies for individual schools or for small groups of schools. In half of the *smaller* county boroughs, however, this is not the case. It is more in evidence in the larger (200,000) authorities, most of which could in 1966 be regarded as firmly under Labour control.

Many chief education officers—indeed a majority—in Labour authorities with few or no governing bodies in any real sense mentioned the determined resistance of their councillors towards any system that might detract from their prerogatives as elected representatives of the people. Co-opted outsiders were sometimes regarded with suspicion, and it was held that it would be embarrassing if governing bodies with numbers of non-elected members took decisions or made representations not in line with the council's official policy. This insistence on the primacy of the democratically elected member, and the associated reluctance to give appointed or co-opted outsiders a share in positions of power or influence, is of long standing in local government. Reservations along these lines were expressed, for example, by W. G. Cove in the House of Commons on 9 March 1944[1] when discussion was taking place on those clauses of the Education Bill concerned with the establishment of managing and governing bodies. Such views may be based on an unduly narrow concept of public participation and exaggerated fears of what non-elected persons might do to thwart the will of the people's representatives,

[1] Hansard, H. C. Debates, Vol. 397, Fifth Series, 1943–44, 9 March 1944.

but they are still very much alive in some areas. There was less evidence to support the view that Conservative-minded authorities actively encourage governing bodies, although there did seem to be a far more general acceptance of the part that school governors should play, and far less suspicion about their basic usefulness. Conservatives also appeared to be far less suspicious of co-opted members, no doubt because—or partly because—they were confident of being able to find people of similar ways of thinking.[2]

There are some striking regional variations in attitude towards governing bodies, of which the most obvious are between Lancashire and Merseyside on the one hand and Yorkshire and the North-East on the other. In the former region, only 4 county boroughs out of 19 have no system of governing bodies in any real sense, and 3 of those 4 at least have a separate meeting of the schools sub-committee, sitting in name as governors. The region contains some of the most solidly Labour boroughs in the country, which are nevertheless ardent supporters of governing bodies. In Yorkshire and the North-East 8 authorities out of 18, with only 4 out of 10 in the West Riding, are in categories A or B. Of these 4, one has economized by replacing individual governing bodies by governing bodies for small groups of schools, with all co-options made from council members, while another is a Conservative authority. In 2 other authorities the chief education officer has been able to give governing bodies a dynamic role of some importance. These latter authorities, however, are exceptional.

Why should there be such contrasting attitudes to school government in socially similar areas like Lancashire and the West Riding? A major factor is certainly the strength of voluntary schools, especially Roman Catholic schools. Many chief education officers stressed the importance of giving county schools parity of status with the denominational schools, which had their own governing bodies, and in county boroughs where 40 or 50 per cent of the children went to church schools, this was regarded as vital for the morale of county schools and their heads.

[2] These findings are in line with those of J. G. Bulpitt in *Party Politics in English Local Government*, 1967.

No other regions present such clear cut differences as Lancashire and Yorkshire. For example, no conclusion can be drawn about Midland county boroughs in general. But the medium-sized county towns and resort towns are predominantly in groups A or B. For the most part they are Conservative or marginally Labour, and none of them is very large. They contain plenty of the most obvious sources of potential governors, professional and retired people and women with time on their hands. Within each main category are found authorities of very different characteristics, and authorities which could be regarded as social or political twins have fundamentally differing outlooks.

Large county borough X has no governing bodies because it is held that they would be a waste of time and that it would be impossible to find enough people to serve on them; large county borough Y regards governing bodies as an essential part of the education service and has no difficulty at all in recruiting governors. Small authority A claims that there is no use for governing bodies because it has only eight county secondary schools and the chief education officer can get to any of them within ten minutes; small authority B thinks that without an independent body of governors the heads would be entirely at the mercy of the education office.

History and inertia go some way to explaining these differences, and every type of system is justified on the grounds that 'We've always (or never) had governing bodies and see no reason to change'. More important, especially when a critical eye is being cast over current practices, is the personality and interest of the chief education officer, and in particular the extent to which he can get his own way with his committee. Without doubt, the authorities in which governors are likely to play a most active part are those in which the chief education officer favours their doing so. More than one, incidentally, said that he was using the development of a system of comprehensive schools as an opportunity to provide individual schools or pairs of schools with their own governing bodies.

COUNTY BOROUGHS WITH ONE GOVERNING BODY FOR ALL SCHOOLS

No limits are imposed by law on the number of schools that can be grouped under a single body of governors. Some authorities go to the extreme of grouping *all* their secondary schools under a body composed wholly of education committee members. Such a nominal governing body tends to be larger than usual, consisting of about two dozen members (although in 3 authorities the membership is respectively 13, 12 and 9). A dozen of the 20 authorities in this Category D provide for co-option from outside the ranks of the education committee, but in six others co-optative places are filled by education committee members. The chairmanship of the governing body is often restricted, to judge from the 9 authorities for which information is available. In five cases it is held by the chairman of the education committee, in two by the vice-chairman, and in another by the vice-chairman of the secondary schools sub-committee. The last authority has a strange system in which the governing body re-forms itself seven times, once for each secondary school, and on each occasion elects a different chairman, all seven meetings being held consecutively.

Meetings tend to be held at more frequent intervals in these authorities than in those operating more highly developed systems of school government. Of 15 of these authorities 11 held monthly meetings. The frequency of attendance by heads varies. In 4 small authorities with 7 or 8 schools all heads attend all meetings of the governing body: in others each head attends once a term or every nine months: in one authority with 23 schools 5 heads attend each meeting, and elsewhere heads attend 'when necessary' or 'rarely'. In order to forge closer links between the schools and the governing body, a number of authorities have arranged for governors to visit their schools in turn. There are also instances of meetings being held in first one school and then another.

THE COUNTIES AND GROUPING

Grouping of schools assumes much less extreme forms in the counties, of which almost half (22 out of 45) had individual governing bodies throughout; 20 had a mixture of individual governing bodies and governing bodies for groups of schools; and 3 had only the latter. As is shown in the table below, individual governing bodies are found mainly in the counties without divisional executives which are, generally speaking, the smaller counties. But they are also found in some large counties. A mixture of practice is found in counties at every level of size and population.

	Individual Governing Bodies	Mixed	Grouped Throughout
A Counties with no Divisional Executive	15	7	–
B Counties with some Divisional Executives	4	7	I
C Counties wholly or mainly covered by Divisional Executives	3	6	2
	22	20	3

(Excepted Districts[3] ignored)

Grouping in category A counties generally occurs in towns, or in respect of schools on the same site. This is also true for category B, but it is not the whole story, as there are variations between the directly administered parts of the county and the divisional executive areas. In the former individual governing bodies are the norm, with a mixture of practice found in the divisional executives. No common pattern could be traced for counties in category C; 2 counties followed an overall policy of governing bodies for individual schools.

---

[3] An excepted district is a borough, or urban district which, as its name implies, is 'excepted' from certain administrative arrangements elsewhere determined by a county authority (as, for example, arrangements for managing and governing bodies).

The policy of grouping throughout found in the 3 remaining counties had been introduced deliberately but for differing reasons in each case. One county had adopted an overall policy of small groups, with an optimum number of 3 schools in each, to satisfy demands for parity of esteem, to give governors an insight into the needs of a wider area, and to solve the problems caused by a shortage of governors. In the second county grouping seems to be a natural concomitant to the policy of developing multilateral units comprising a number of schools on the same or different sites. The governing bodies are large, often containing 20 or so members and, it is claimed, can take a broad and balanced view of the needs of all their schools. Each has well-developed sub-committees which have a special concern with individual schools; it is thus closely acquainted with the latter and with issues affecting the area as a whole. In some divisions of this county there are only three or four governing bodies, and it is not easy to see how the two outlooks of governors and divisional executives can be distinguished. The third county has traditionally grouped primary and secondary schools together on the grounds that the same bodies should be concerned with children's needs throughout their school life. This system has attracted a good deal of criticism, especially from those who think that primary and secondary schools have little in common and that it is difficult for the same body to make an equally effective contribution at both levels. Governing bodies in this authority tend to have consecutive meetings for primary and secondary school matters, and in some other areas grouping is on a horizontal rather than a vertical basis. It should be noted that there are authorities which ensure continuity of interest and concern by ensuring that some secondary school governors are nominated by the managing bodies of contributory primary schools.

The great majority of chief education officers asserted that they were in favour of individual governing bodies or governing bodies for small groups of schools. They did not share the views expressed by some of their colleagues in the county boroughs that such systems were administratively too expensive, or that suitable people could not be found in sufficient numbers to serve as governors. Even in some of the largest counties individual governing bodies were not seen as an intolerable burden, save by a few divisional officers. Chief education officers felt that they might have to acquiesce in grouping schools if a minor authority strongly favoured this, and it was said that excepted districts were too much inclined to favour large groups and to ignore the county's expressed preference for individual governing bodies. However, this is not substantiated by evidence from 30 excepted districts. 14 of these have individual governing bodies; 11 have governing bodies for one or two schools; and in only 5 are there more than two schools per governing body.

HEADS' VIEWS ON GROUPING

The heads' and university governors' questionnaires provide two further sources of information and views on differing patterns of school government. Information and views do not always go together, however, and the strongest views are sometimes expressed by those who have had no experience of schools being grouped together for governing purposes, but who find the idea itself objectionable.

As explained elsewhere heads' opinions were canvassed by means of two questionnaires, one issued to all members of the Headmasters' Association and the Association of Headmistresses and the other to a national sample of all other heads of secondary schools. These will be referred to as the HMM questionnaire and the NSH questionnaire respectively.

Respondents to the HMM questionnaire were predominantly heads of grammar schools with their own governing bodies. Of 176 in the counties only 36 shared with other schools; and in county boroughs, where grouping is more common, only 46 out of 122.

Of the heads who shared a governing body, 22 (10 in the counties and 12 in the county boroughs) indicated that they did so with a brother or sister school of the same type and on the same or a neighbouring site. 28 heads, all in county boroughs, said they shared with a number of schools. Quite often positive enthusiasm was expressed for sharing with a brother, sister or neighbour school, on the grounds that common problems can be shared and governors' interests broadened. Helpful and positive comparisons can be made, and the demands made on governors are not so great as to diminish their interest in either school. Many heads emphasize that the acceptability of sharing depends very much on their personal relationships with the other head involved. Reservations are made by some headmistresses who state that their governors tend to regard the affairs of their brother school as more important, and by heads who dislike having to discuss some of their domestic problems in front of their colleagues. Arrangements are made in some authorities for heads to withdraw when delicate matters affecting another school are being discussed.

There is less enthusiasm for grouping a selective and a non-selective school together, although the logic of this arrangement may be accepted when the two schools are to be amalgamated at some future date. Each head may be suspicious that the other school is being favoured, and heads of both selective and non-selective schools replied to this effect. However, one head in a mixed group of three said that he used to deplore grouping, but now strongly approved of the practice: parity of esteem was observed, and heads' reports were received with equal interest. Where four or more schools were grouped, heads' comments were very forthright and invariably adverse. They maintained that grouping to this extent diminished the governors' interest; that there was no time to deal adequately with the affairs of any one school; that any attempt to increase governors' involvement was regarded as an attempt to curry favour at the expense of other schools; and that irrelevant, invidious and embarrassing comparisons were made. A practice everywhere condemned was that of holding meetings at the Town Hall instead of in the schools, with heads either waiting outside a committee room (as one of them put it, 'like naughty boys') for their few minutes with the governing body, and kept unaware of any general matters already discussed; or else let in to sit through a string of boring reports or discussions of confidential matters affecting other schools.

Respondents to the NSH questionnaire were virtually all heads of non-selective schools, since the schools already approached through the HMM questionnaire were removed from the total population of secondary schools from which the sample was drawn. By and large their reactions were similar to those already described, but some interesting points emerge from an examination of the replies of heads serving in county boroughs with a single governing body serving all secondary schools. Those who had had no experience of any other system were equally divided between supporting and opposing their authority's policy. 14 were identified, however, who had served as heads in schools with their own governing body. Of these, all but 3 preferred this latter arrangement.

THE MEMBERSHIP OF GOVERNING BODIES

Instruments of government invariably provide for places on governing bodies to be filled by representatives of the local education authority and, where this is appropriate in the counties, by representatives also of minor authorities and of a divisional executive or excepted district. Normally, for local education authority places the county councillor or alderman for the area submits names to the education committee for approval. Local people, preferably having a connexion with the school and otherwise well known, are usually nominated. Sometimes there are hints that councillors are too inclined to find governors only from among their own cronies or party supporters. In most counties there is little attempt to get a majority of councillors or education committee members on governing bodies; simple arithmetic shows that this would be fruitless, as there may not be enough members to go round the schools. Indeed, some governing bodies have no such members at all. In one county, for example, of the 16 comprehensive and grammar schools, 9 had no education committee member on their governing bodies. No figures were available for secondary modern schools. In part of another county, only 2 out of 24 governing bodies included a member of the education committee.

Minor local authorities are said by many chief education officers to be inclined to restrict nominations to their own ranks, and this claim is supported by some lists of governing bodies showing a high proportion of councillors. This means that, when political control of a minor authority changes hands, there may be a considerable turnover of the membership of governing bodies. This is said by heads to be against the interest of the schools, whilst another recurrent complaint they make is that councillors are notoriously bad attenders because of the multiplicity of their commitments.

When a local education authority thinks it necessary to allow representation to every minor authority, however small, governing bodies can be large and unwieldly, sometimes having as many as 20 members. In the great majority of both divisional executives (93 per cent) and excepted districts (82 per cent), more than half of their members served also on governing bodies, while in the remainder there was at least some overlap of membership.

The composition of governing bodies in one excepted district illustrates the tendency for minor authorities to nominate only their own members. It also shows how representation of the local education authority may be subordinated to that of the excepted district.

COMPOSITION OF GOVERNING BODIES IN ONE EXCEPTED DISTRICT

The extent to which membership of governing bodies in some county boroughs is restricted, either through the practice of grouping or the stipulation in instruments that some or all representative governors must be members of the authority had already been shown. Discussions with chief education officers suggested that, even when instruments did not require it, councillors and education committee members often made sure that they occupied

Governing Body	Borough Aldermen	Representatives Councillors	Others	County Aldermen	Representatives Councillors	Others	Co-opted Members
A	4	4	0	1 B.A.	1 C.C.	0	1 Cllr. 1 U.Rep.
B	1	6	1	1 B.A.	1 C.C.	0	2
C	2	5	0	0	2 C.C.	1	2
D	1	5	1	0	1 C.C. 1 B.C.	1	2
E	1	4	2	0	2 B.C.	1	2
F	0	6	1	1 C.A.	1 C.C.	1	2

B.A. Borough Aldermen   C.A. County Alderman   B.C. Borough Councillor   C.C. County Councillor   U.Rep. University Representative

72 seats were occupied by 48 people:

    1 sat on 4 governing bodies
    2 sat on 3 governing bodies
    17 sat on 2 governing bodies
    28 sat on 1 governing body

a good proportion of governors' seats. Several chief education officers and heads said that co-optative places were frequently used to reward party supporters, and not to secure the services of 'persons with interest and experience in education', as prescribed in many instruments. This sort of assertion is difficult to check, but it is too widespread to be disregarded completely.

The extent to which the membership of governing bodies is composed of councillors and education committee members is illustrated by the following data relating to 4 authorities.

I

Governing Body	Representative Governors		
	Education Committee Members	Other Councillors	Non-Councillors
A	4	4	4
B	5	2	5
C	4	4	4
D	4	3	5

II

Governing Body	Representative Governors			Co-opted Governors
	Ed. Committee Members	Other Councillors	Non-Councillors	
A	4	1	2	3
B	4	–	3	3

Note. In this LEA the Instruments stipulated that there were to be at least 2 EC members on each GB.

III

Governing Body	Representative Governors		
	Education Committee Members	Other Councillors	Non-Councillors
A	7 (2 Co-opted)	1	8
B	7 (3 Co-opted)	2	7
C	8 (3 Co-opted)	1	7

IV

Governing Body	Representative Governors			Nominated Governors
	Ed. Committee Members	Other Councillors	Non-Councillors	
A	2	2	7	1
B	2	1	8	1
C	2	5	4	1
D	3	2	6	1
E	4	4	3	1
F	4	–	7	1
G	1	3	7	1
H	1	–	10	1

Although the above tables relate only to a small number of authorities they provide enough information to indicate that, however restrictive some county boroughs may be in their practices, there are others where non-councillors comprise a large proportion of the membership of governing bodies or are even in the majority. The argument advanced in some small county boroughs that the principle of public accountability necessitates that there should be a majority of elected members on all governing bodies is certainly not generally acted upon. The value of the service the elected member can give is not of course in question. Chief education officers, heads and other governors attach great importance to having a member of the education committee on governing bodies, so that there is a direct link between the schools and the authority. In the counties it is often considered a weakness that so many governing bodies do not have this link.

THE CHAIRMANSHIP

Chairmanships of governing bodies are much more open in counties than in county boroughs, where their restriction to members of the authority is frequently laid down in the instruments of government. In counties, and more particularly in the directly administered areas, the election of chairman is regarded as a matter entirely for the individual governing body to determine. Where the board contains a member of the education committee or the county council, he may well be elected to the chair, but there is certainly no rule that this practice should be followed. In some of the larger divisionally administered counties more importance is attached to the chairman being a member of the authority or the divisional executive, and in those counties where politics influence the composition of governing bodies chairmanships may be shared on a pro rata basis, or be in the pocket of the majority party.

Apart from those county boroughs with one governing body for all schools, in just under half the remainder chairmanships of governing bodies are restricted to members of the authority or of the education committee. Authorities with individual governing bodies impose this restriction less than those with governing bodies for groups of schools, but even so a third in the former category follow this practice. Where formal limitations are not imposed in the instruments of government the chairmanships of governing bodies may be restricted by the majority party retaining *all* chairmanships in its hands, and possibly through their being further limited to members of the education committee. In politically marginal county boroughs chairmanships may be shared. For example, in one such authority the chairmanships of 8 governing bodies had been allocated as follows:

4 were filled with Labour nominees, comprising 3 aldermen and 1 councillor, all on the education committee.

4 were filled with Conservative nominees, comprising 1 alderman and 1 councillor on the education committee, 1 councillor not on the education committee and (by way of experiment) a chairman from outside the ranks of the authority.

A school whose chairman of governors is on the education committee is often considered to be particularly well placed, as a chairman can speak with more authority than a rank and file governor. One of the area studies confirmed that both heads and governors thought that their schools would be at a disadvantage without a direct personal link with the education committee; there was no evidence to suggest that the independence of governing bodies was thus jeopardized, and it was generally agreed that members of an authority could be very active in championing their own schools. Some disenchanted heads, however, thought their chairmen tended to speak with one voice at governors' meetings and with another in committee.

Although chairmen are normally elected annually, there is a great deal of evidence that, in the counties particularly, the same people are reappointed year after year and that there is little injection of new blood. This is also true in some county boroughs. While there are obvious advantages in a chairman's holding office for more than one year, it does not seem desirable that he should be able to remain in the chair unchallenged until he drops dead— as happened in one area studied. Elsewhere chairmen in their 70s or 80s were encountered, and a story heard of one governing body which tried to appoint a new chairman, only to find that the current occupant, who had held the seat for 20 years, refused to vacate it and continued to carry on his own correspondence with the authority! Some authorities, but very few, have a rotation system for chairmen, and prohibit the same person from serving for more than a set number of years. By this means a sitting chairman can be replaced without hard feelings, while heads do not have to contend with a bad or ageing chairman year in year out. At the opposite extreme, heads may have to get used to a new chairman almost every year, as a consequence of chairmanships being voted on a political basis. This does not encourage the development of anything more than a formal relationship between head and chairman, and does not give the latter long enough in the post to make himself of much use to the school.

Realization that continual change of chairmen is not in the best interests of the schools has caused political leaders in some authorities to argue against having a clean sweep every year, and to adjust the membership of governing bodies accordingly.

PARTY POLITICS AND RECRUITMENT OF GOVERNORS

The political basis of appointments to governing bodies is a matter which not unnaturally arouses strong passions. At their most extreme the arguments for and against are roughly as follows:

(1) The primacy of the elected representatives of the people demands that not only the ultimate authority, the local education authority, but also all subordinate bodies should reflect the people's will in their composition. Governing bodies have no right to take decisions which might embarrass the authority or be contrary to its declared policy; their place in the local administrative structure can be justified only if they are composed of elected representatives chosen in accordance with party strength on the authority.

(2) Education should not be regarded as a matter of party politics, and it would be better served by men and women of good will who devoted themselves to the schools' interests without reference to decisions taken elsewhere by political parties. An identification of governing bodies with the views of the authority results in the irrelevant introduction of political arguments. There can exist a general consensus of opinion about what is best for a

school, and this consensus should be the paramount consideration for governors.

Stated in this form the arguments may appear unrealistic and naïve, and more convincing cases for and against a political basis to school government can be made in less extreme form. Nevertheless, these two conflicting points of view are useful in understanding the range and variety of opinion expressed both in counties and county boroughs.

According to the chief education officers of county authorities, politics play no discernible part in the appointment of governors in the majority of counties. It is only in the larger and the more heavily populated that they are said to be apparent. This picture of apolitical innocence in the more rural areas may be misleading for several reasons. Nominations are in the hands of local county councillors or members of minor authorities. Many county councillors are returned unopposed or do not stand on overtly party political grounds. In turn, the recruitment of school governors is based on personal considerations and not upon party affiliations, which may not exist. One result, according to some chief education officers, is that governors were frequently drawn from 'traditional' leaders of rural communities, with little account taken of other sources. They express concern over the extent to which governing bodies, even of secondary modern schools, may be overwhelmingly middle-class in composition in some areas and contain nobody who has been educated in a local education authority school. There is, when nominations are on a mainly personal basis, a tendency to choose governors who are broadly of the same way of thinking as oneself, and one suspects that the term 'politics' is used only to describe the views of discordant elements. A telling example comes from one county where a newly elected county councillor did not renominate for service as governors such people as the local doctor and the squire's lady, but put forward the names of his own supporters who suffered the handicap of being young (some, moreover, actually had children in local schools) and 'foreigners'—i.e. they had not lived in the same village all their lives. This was thought by some leading members of the authority to be bringing politics into local government.

There is also evidence that some minor authorities make appointments to governing bodies on a political basis and to restrict nominations to their own members. This may express a natural, if at time exaggerated, desire to ensure that local councils are able to make their views clearly felt on educational matters, especially in cases of differences with county policy, whether actual or proposed. Urban districts and non-county boroughs are more overtly political than many counties and may, if politically opposed to the county, be particularly concerned to keep a firm hand on nominations.

Nearly half of the chief education officers of the 58 county boroughs with governing bodies for individual schools or groups of schools claimed that politics did not enter into the appointment of governors. Where it did, it was more likely in authorities which brought large numbers of schools together for government purposes.

COUNTY BOROUGHS (58) WITH GOVERNING BODIES FOR INDIVIDUAL SCHOOLS OR GROUPS OF SCHOOLS

Opinions of chief education officers on political basis	County Boroughs with governing bodies for individual schools	County Boroughs with governing bodies for small groups of schools	County Boroughs with governing bodies for large groups of schools
Non-political	11	12	3
Political	8	10	8
No opinion	2	3	1
Total	21	25	12

Where political considerations openly determined the composition of governing bodies, the usual practice was for the parties to share seats in proportion to their strengths on the council. The arguments advanced for this practice are closely related to those for packing governing bodies with councillors or members of the education committee: that, in order to reflect the verdict of the people, the composition of governing bodies would be identical with that of the elected authority.

The political basis of appointments to governorships was criticized by a substantial minority to the HMM questionnaire and the NSH questionnaire

	HMM questionnaire		NSH questionnaire	
	All heads	Heads critical of political bias	All heads	Heads critical of political bias
Counties	132	46 (27%)	238	58 (24%)
County Boroughs	76	19 (25%)	119	45 (38%)
	208	65	357	103

Some heads were opposed entirely to a political element on governing bodies; others accepted its inevitability if elected representatives were to be allowed some direct oversight of publicly maintained schools, but held that some governors should be drawn from other sources. Political nominations were often thought to result in the recruitment of governors with no apparent interest in education, and a corresponding exclusion of others better qualified to serve.

Similar criticisms were made by university governors. Among factors hampering the appointment of suitable people, the political basis for appointment was mentioned nearly three times as often as any other. Criticism was especially severe when it was felt that it led to the predominance of limited social and occupational groups. On the other side, it was sometimes said that it could produce governing bodies drawn from a broad and varied cross-section of the community and with a real concern for the school.

A number of the local politicians and chairmen of governing bodies interviewed in the course of the area studies themselves mentioned the grave disadvantages of exclusive recruitment from the ranks of party members. At the same time they thought that active party workers included people interested in the community and aware of the problems of local government and administration, and that within a local party would be found people from many different backgrounds.

PARENTAL REPRESENTATION

The field studies reported here were completed before the present trend to increase parental representation on managing and governing bodies had got under way.

As might be expected, heads differed in their attitudes towards parents serving as governors, the results of the questionnaire studies being as follows:

Views of Heads on parent governors

HMA/AHM members in county schools	Approve	Dis-approve	Unde-cided	No answer	Total
Heads in counties					
with parent governors	29	4	23	10	66
without parent governors	12	19	9	19	59
Heads in county boroughs					
with parent governors	11	7	9	5	32
without parent governors	4	15	3	13	35
National Sample of Heads					
Heads in counties					
with parent governors	51	18	21	10	100
without parent governors	30	31	18	26	105
Heads in county boroughs					
with parent governors	16	5	4	10	35
without parent governors	27	26	5	6	64

It will be noted in both surveys that heads with parent governors favour them more than those without such experience; and that heads in the NSH sample (mainly heads of non-selective schools) are more favourably disposed to parent governors than those in the HMA/AHM survey (mainly heads of selective schools).

Some heads complained that parents did not treat governors' transactions as confidential; others that they were too closely linked with the school to be objective; and yet others that parent governors asked for special favours or that their presence might be embarrassing when, for example, staffing questions were being discussed. On the other hand some heads maintained that parent governors could have a deeper knowledge of the working of the schools and a greater interest and sympathy than other governors. The very fact that their approach to the schools was different was in itself valuable. They could well act as leaven in an elderly lump.

A major question is whether parents should have *formal* representation. This exists in 9 counties and 11 county boroughs, in some cases through representative, in others through co-optative governors. Where a school has a parent-teacher association or parents' association, this body will normally put forward a name acceptable to the head. But since such an association is not encouraged in all schools, there is not always an organized body of parents to be represented. In these circumstances it may be questioned whether parental 'representation' is possible. Can one parent represent the interests of others unless there is an organized body of parents?

In authorities where there is no specific provision for parental representation, opinion was almost equally divided over its value. Some chief education officers felt that formal representation of parents nominated by parent-teacher associations or parent associations might be dangerous, should the representative regard himself in any way as a delegate. There is, however, little evidence to show that parents nominated by associations regard themselves as delegates or are considered by heads to be any more awkward than other governors.

The few university governors who mentioned parental representation all thought it was a practice which should be generally adopted. It was probably the most effective way of ensuring that the voice of parents was heard in educational circles, and it showed that parents' views were sought and considered seriously.

UNIVERSITY REPRESENTATIVES ON GOVERNING BODIES

308 replies were received from a total of 371 questionnaires despatched to governors appointed by universities.

University teachers in Departments or Institutes of Education	49
University teachers in other Departments	190
University graduates recruited through Convocation or a similar body	63
Senior administrative staff	6
	308

Virtually all universities were represented in the sample. The only exceptions were some of the newest foundations which had not had time to attend to this matter. The speed with which some new universities had got off the mark was most impressive, as was also the keenness to approach them shown by neighbouring local education authorities. It is clear that only a minority of university representatives could be described as specialists in education; university representatives who were neither university teachers nor administrators were appointed by 6 universities, locally resident graduates furnishing a convenient source of supply for governing bodies of schools situated some way from the university. Most universities nominated governors only for neighbouring authorities, but some were also involved, because of traditional connexions, with schools at a greater distance. This was particularly noticeable in the case of Oxford, Cambridge and London.

Chief education officers with experience of university governors welcomed them. They were considered to be a great help to the heads and to be valuable because they were not involved in local politics and because they possessed a knowledge of academic problems. They were appreciated particularly where universities had made a special effort to provide a large number from their staff and thus strengthen the link between themselves and local schools. Reservations came from chief education officers of authorities situated some way from a university, who found that places were often unfilled, that university governors were bad attenders, and that if a local graduate was appointed he might have no special contribution to make. In their turn university teachers on distant governing bodies sometimes admitted that they did not attend as often as they should, and that they were out of touch with local feeling. It was also suggested by a few chief education officers that junior university teachers were wrapped up in their own research and would not carry weight with a body of 'potent, grave and reverend signors', while more senior people were too busy with other commitments. But these opinions are not borne out by the experience of most authorities with university teachers on their governing bodies.

The great majority of university governors thought that they had a special contribution to make, and that they had adequate opportunity to make it. This was slightly less true of the graduate representatives, and less true in county boroughs than in counties and the Inner London Education Authority.

Percentage of university representatives thinking they can make special contribution

	All	University teachers	Graduate representatives	Total numbers
	%	%	%	
Counties	83	85	67	190
County Boroughs	68	74	42	64
Inner London Education Authority	80	88	72	54

The special contribution most frequently referred to is that of being able to place professional knowledge at the head's disposal. In more general terms university governors think that their broader outlook and independence from local political life and

the local education authority ('I can't be got at by the chief education officer') can be extremely valuable, especially when it is a
matter of enlisting support for a head. Some university governors
find that they come to be regarded as confidants to the head, who is
prepared to talk to them privately about staffing and matters which
he would be reluctant to mention at a governors' meeting, or even
to discuss with individual elected representatives. They feel they
can put the head's case for him when other governors fail to
realize the educational import of their own proposals and when
the head might feel that he needs to be circumspect.

The relatively few criticisms expressed by university governors
are found mainly where the local education authority takes a
restrictive view of school government in general, or where they
are regarded with some suspicion because they are the only outsiders. One such governor was disillusioned because deliberations
had been concerned with such topics as the type of paint to be
used on walls, and the suitability of the facilities given to the local
youth club. Another claimed that the authority sought to minimize
his role and to convey a firm impression that a university governor
was an interfering outsider.

Generally, however, university governors seemed to be reasonably satisfied that work on governing bodies was worthwhile. But
it should be borne in mind that the evidence came from serving
university governors, and that there are no direct means of telling
how many previous governors had resigned or not offered themselves for reappointment because they became disillusioned or
thought the entire system valueless. However, nearly 75 per cent
of the sample had served for more than three years and thus had
had at least one opportunity of withdrawing from office when
governing bodies were reconstituted. Even if tenure amounted to
no more than six years, which was exceeded by just over half of
the sample, this could be regarded as a satisfactory term of office.

The heads interviewed in the course of the area studies were on
the whole greatly in favour of university governors, although one
had found his 'incoherent, idealistic, and unhelpful', and the poor
attendance of others was also noticed. However, it was claimed

Years on Governing Body	Oxbridge	London and Older Civic Universities	New Universities
	%	%	%
1–3	24	26	24
4–6	20	19	40
7–9	—	13	2
10–14	28	21	22
15–19	16	10	6
20	12	11	6
	100	100	100

that when spasmodic attenders did turn up their views were listened to with respect, although one or two were thought to be so different from the other governors and to make so little effort to appreciate their point of view that they became completely isolated. Sometimes heads of secondary modern schools could not see much point in university representation on the boards of their schools—and here their views coincided with those of some university governors themselves—but even these felt that, as their schools developed extended courses and, in particular post 'O' level work, the case for university representation would become stronger.

TEACHING STAFF REPRESENTATION

At the time of this study teachers were excluded from being governors of their own school and normally, indeed, of any school in their own local education authority. Only in very few authorities is there specific provision for any form of teaching staff representation. Some other authorities, in accordance with the general direction in the Command Paper that 'the interests of the teaching staff of the school or schools should be reflected in the composition of the governing body', allow teachers from other schools inside or outside the authority to serve.

In general chief education officers argued that teacher representation is unnecessary since the head is expected to act as spokesman for his staff. For him to have a member of staff, or even a teacher from another school or authority serving as a governor would be an embarrassment. Interviews with heads in the main supported these objections, although some thought there should be a closer link between the staff and the governors. Some suggested that senior members of staff might be allowed to attend part of governors' meetings, to contribute to discussion or explain the needs and work of their department. Senior members might also be involved with governors in staff appointments. Such practices are already found un-officially in some instances.

In those cases where university governors mentioned staff representation, it was to suggest that teachers would make a useful addition to the governing body. Some suggested that a head, far from acting as a spokesman for his staff, might obstruct communication between staff and governors. Informal means were not considered sufficient to overcome this blockage, and formal provision for staff representation was therefore necessary. Some thought that a parallel might be drawn between staff representation on the governing body of a school and staff representation at universities, colleges of education and further education institutions.

This was not the view of the chief education officer in one of the two counties where provision was made, customarily on the nomination of the head, for the representation of teaching staff. He did not regard it as a first step towards academic self-government, since he held that an institution such as a secondary school requires a hierarchical structure with authority stemming from one man.

There are strong arguments in favour of moving away from such a concept of head/staff relations. Schools are organizations of increasing size and complexity and the role of the head is becoming more managerial, with special emphasis being placed on the development of effective patterns of communication, consultation and decision-making. The case for a considerable measure of staff participation in the government of colleges of education was argued with cogency in the Weaver report, *The Government of Colleges of Education* (1966), and it has been substantially accepted in institutions of higher and further education. An essential feature of this autonomy is direct representation of the academic staff on the governing body. There are already indications that schools will move in the same direction. One head interviewed thought that there was room for academic sub-committees of teaching staff who could report direct to the governors. This had, for example, been tried successfully at one school for the distribution of scholarship money and for the arrangements for a Sixth Form Open Day, and could be usefully extended to other spheres.

The practical implications of staff representation have been studied in some depth in one authority where teachers serve on governing bodies for groups of schools. The procedure for the appointment of the teacher representatives is interesting and probably unique. A representative must be a teacher in one of the authority's secondary schools, but he cannot serve on the board governing the school at which he works. There are two teachers on each board (8 boards in all), making 16 teacher representatives. One teacher who serves as a representative on two boards is a cooptative member of the education committee.

At one time the professional associations in the city, the N.U.T. and the Joint Four,[4] had each nominated one candidate to each board, and these were normally appointed unopposed. Now the procedure is for teachers in each school to nominate one of their number to a panel of nominees for places on governing bodies other than those serving their own schools. The teachers in each group of schools then hold an election by secret ballot for their two representative governors. This procedure, of course, puts nominations in the hands of the staff-rooms rather than the teacher associations. Persons appointed as teacher representatives were normally deputy heads or heads of department, who would have considerable experience and knowledge of the administrative as well as the educational problems which schools have to face.

[4] That is, the Associations of Headmasters, Headmistresses, Assistant Masters and Assistant Mistresses of Secondary Schools which, in some policy matters act in concert.

Only two heads interviewed did not favour the system, their objection being that the authority in general accorded too much respect to teachers. The rest welcomed the knowledge of other schools and of other types of education which the teacher representatives brought to governors' discussions. They were also in sympathy with any governors who came to their support as the teacher representatives did. The latter felt that they were representatives of their schools and also of the profession as a whole. Most of them felt it their duty to support the head in his demands for facilities and resources, and to stand up for the rights of the school staff against criticisms levelled at them by the other governors or by outsiders. Members of the authority itself, although generally against the principle of cooption, had always accepted the representation of teachers on governing bodies and quoted the Command Paper as the reason for following this practice; they could hardly have been aware that they are one of the few authorities which followed its directions so faithfully!

OLD SCHOLAR REPRESENTATION

It was found that relatively few governing bodies had specific provision for old scholar representation. Where it existed it was generally welcomed and certainly aroused much less antagonism than parental representation.

HMA/AHM members in county schools	Counties	County Boroughs
Number of heads in sample	132	76
Number of heads with o.s. as governors	53	34
Number of heads approving of o.s. governors	38	15
Number of heads disapproving	10	4
Number of heads undecided	5	15
National Sample of Heads		
Number of heads	195	99
Number of heads with o.s. as governors	21	40
Number of heads approved of o.s. as governors	15	23
Number of heads disapproving	5	10
Number of heads undecided	1	7

Old scholars are found on governing bodies both as formally appointed representatives and as those who are appointed or co-opted as individuals. In both cases heads appreciated their presence. Old scholars can, it seems, be expected to maintain their interest in the school and they show greater keenness than other governors. But reservations are expressed by some heads who think that there should be a decent interval before a former pupil becomes a governor (one was reluctant to have an old boy governor under the age of 40, which seems excessively cautious) or that a man should not become a governor while his old head is still in office. It is also thought that, since schools are changing and developing rapidly, often in very unexpected directions, such governors would have no greater knowledge of their own schools than other governors. Indeed, one of the main reasons why some heads were against having former pupils as governors was because they harked back to the good old days when they themselves were at school, and because they tended to oppose change.

WIDENING THE AREA OF RECRUITMENT

The main factor hampering the appointment of governors with ability and enthusiasm is quite clearly the political, especially where few or no outsiders are recruited. This is borne out by both heads and university governors, and is confirmed in general terms by some chief education officers. The argument that no political appointments should be made to governing bodies is, of course, quite unrealistic. On the other hand, the experience of the counties and of some county boroughs does not support the view that only the political parties can provide a sufficient number of interested persons to serve on governing bodies. Another and related restrictive factor is the tendency in county boroughs for places on governing bodies to be filled largely by councillors and members of the education committee.

Even where appointments are not made on an exclusively political or 'elected representatives' basis, governing bodies may have an unduly narrow social base, whether this mainly consists of miners, as in some areas or, as in others, the 'wealthy, leisured and retired who have little sympathy with the problems of a maintained grammar school'. Elsewhere, it is not thought necessary to recruit women governors in any number, even for girls' and mixed schools. Particularly in politically static areas, governors are inclined to continue in office indefinitely, and appointments of younger men and women with children of their own and who are receptive to new ideas, are regarded with suspicion. There is the case of a woman university governor who went to her first meeting at the girls' high school to find herself the only woman there apart from the headmistress, and to be greeted with 'Aren't you awfully young to be a governor?' She was 42 at the time.

The inability of members of governing bodies to claim their expenses is considered by chief education officers and governors as a deterrent to service. It is claimed too that many ordinary working people cannot afford the loss of earnings entailed by taking time off during the day to attend meetings and to see the school at work. An unusual illustration of this was given by a chief education officer who said that in one or two areas governing bodies consisted almost entirely of steelworkers on night shift. If service on governing bodies is to be taken seriously, it is essential that those involved should not have to suffer financial hardship. But no travelling expenses or compensation for loss of earnings can at present be paid. There is one authority which has arrived at a working solution to this problem by constituting all governing bodies as sub-committees of the education committee.

There are authorities which enlarge their area of choice by advertising for would-be governors in the local press. Applicants have to submit details of their qualifications and experience, and a final decision is taken by the education committee. In one largely working-class authority there are four or five applications for every vacancy, and the standard of governors is said to be correspondingly high. This seems to be an admirable method of enlisting public support and interest in the schools, and it is surprising that so few authorities have made use of it.

SCHOOL GOVERNMENT IN TRANSITION

Within the framework of the research project two series of studies of Outer London Boroughs were undertaken. The first was in 1966 when all were visited, and the second took the form of return visits to four authorities only. These return visits were undertaken in 1968. In addition two studies were undertaken of local education authorities in other parts of the country which were found to have recently remodelled their systems of school government.

It is, of course, important to realize that the picture we have drawn of the situation in 1966 cannot be taken as descriptive of what exists now, nor as indicative of what the future may bring. The past seven years have seen a growing interest in all aspects of school and college government and this interest is only just beginning to find expression in many local education authorities.

The Outer London Boroughs. The London Government Act, 1963, did not require the new authorities set up to change existing procedures in respect of school management and government. Section 31 (7) of the Act states:

In the case of any school maintained immediately before 1st April 1965 by a local education authority who in consequence of this Act will not continue to maintain it on and after that date—

(a) any instrument or rules of management or articles of government made by an order under section 17 of the said Act of 1944 and any arrangement made under section 20 of that Act, being an order or arrangement in force immediately before that date, shall continue in force on and after that date, subject to any further such order or arrangement . . . as if—

(i) any reference therein to that local education authority were a reference to the authority by whom . . . the school falls to be maintained on and after that date . . .

(ii) any reference therein to any other existing local authority, being the council of a metropolitan borough, non-county borough or urban district . . . were a reference . . . to the council of the London borough which includes the area of that existing authority . . .

In Middlesex the characteristic structure of school government operating in the minor authorities had been one of grouped governing bodies on an area basis, although three authorities had individual governing bodies, and two others had a single committee as the governing body for all schools. No area in Middlesex had a system of managing bodies for primary schools, and in four of the boroughs formed from Middlesex the practice of grouping secondary schools on an area basis was being continued. In two areas the new boroughs had disbanded the system of individual governing bodies which had existed in parts of their area, and had created a group system comparable to that found elsewhere. The pervading influence seemed to be the practice existing in these areas before reorganization. Another borough was adopting an interim arrangement for school government until it could take into account the consequences of secondary school reorganization. This authority was continuing the system of grouping schools which had operated in two of the former minor authority areas and had introduced an interim provision of three *ad hoc* sub-committees responsible for school government in another area where hitherto there had been a single body responsible for the government of all county secondary schools. This change, although temporary, showed some recognition of the case for having a governing body rather than a sub-committee system.

Two authorities had been formed within the areas of two administrative counties; in one of these the diversity of practice existing before 1965 presented the new borough with three possible bases of school government, ranging from individual or grouped governing bodies to a single committee. The new borough introduced a system of grouped bodies on a geographical basis. This was thought to be the most efficient and convenient administrative system. Individual bodies were considered to be too expensive in time and manpower, while a single committee would be too anonymous and large. In the other authority the diversity of practice had not been resolved at the time of writing and no policy had been clearly formulated.

In Surrey a characteristic feature had been a joint arrangement combining primary and secondary schools in small groups. All the new boroughs, however, straightway separated school management and government and created distinct managing and governing bodies responsible for groups of schools on an area basis, although one authority had, in addition, a separate body for its grammar schools. The reason given for this special arrangement was that the equivalent school in the area was a voluntary controlled school, and the county grammar school felt it was being badly treated by not having its own governing body.

Of the two new London boroughs which included existing county boroughs, one was continuing its former practice and had not tried to introduce the different systems found in the two minor authorities combined with it. Inside the new borough, indeed, there was a hybrid system of joint managing and governing bodies, grouped managing bodies, grouped governing bodies and individual governing bodies. The other borough had continued the system of area groups for managing and governing bodies, but had provided for governors to serve as managers of contributory primary schools.

In Kent there had been a variety of practices. While there were separate bodies for managing and governing bodies in many areas, some minor authorities preferred grouping and others had individual bodies. In some area grouping was in terms of school type, but elsewhere was on a geographical basis. The two London boroughs formed from the six minor authorities in the Kent area were both proposing to introduce a system of grouped managing and governing bodies for administrative convenience. In one area the difficulties seemed to be clearly related to local interests wishing to maintain the *status quo*.

In Essex the characteristic feature of school management and government was a system of individual governing bodies for secondary schools, and grouped managing bodies for primary schools, although in a few instances primary schools had their own managing bodies.

The overall tendency in the Outer London Boroughs at the time of our first study was, therefore, to favour the grouping of managing and governing bodies. Except in one instance individual governing bodies were survivals from earlier practice. The existence of a single schools sub-committee acting as the managing body of all primary schools is the most significant demonstration of the general feeling in favour of grouping and of ensuring the dominance of the elected councillor or member of the education committee.

In fifteen of the Outer London Boroughs the Council itself had exercised overall control over managing and governing body membership, and party political factors were said to be the most important influence determining the allocation of managerships and governorships. The strength of political feeling in four other boroughs was said to be such as to preclude any consideration of places on managing and governing bodies being filled by people outside political circles. In only one borough were members of the Council not in a majority on managing and governing bodies. Managing and governing bodies were in no sense conceived of as forming separate and distinctive pressure groups, but rather as 'collaborating' pressure groups providing a forum for discussion at school level.

Four new boroughs had university representatives on the governing bodies of selective schools and two boroughs had provision for the co-option of university representatives, if the individual governing body so desired. In general in the Outer London Boroughs there was little evidence of enthusiasm for bringing university representatives on to governing bodies. Only one authority showed interest in outside representation; in this area an experiment was being made in providing for parent-teacher associations to nominate representatives.

Eight authorities reported that party political factors determined the election of the chairmen of managing and governing bodies. The majority party was jealous of their right to secure control through chairmanships. In one area governing bodies were chaired by the Chairman and Vice-Chairman of the Education, the Vice-Chairman of the Schools Sub-Committee and the Chairman of the Buildings Sub-Committee. In another case governing bodies were chaired by the Mayor and Deputy Mayor, the Leader of the Council, and the Chairman of the Education Committee. Such arrangements ensured very close control over the proceedings. One authority went as far as stipulating in its Instruments that the Chairman of the Education Committee should be *ex-officio* on all managing and governing bodies: indeed, one went still further and stipulated both the Chairman and Vice-Chairman of the Education Committee as a double safeguard.

These examples indicate how carefully guarded was the membership of managing and governing bodies in the Outer London Boroughs at the time of the survey. Very great care was being taken to ensure that managing and governing bodies could not take an independent line. It is not unfair to say that the aim was to comply with statutory requirements and little more.

During return visits to four authorities in 1968 attention was focused on local reactions to the grouping of governing bodies and on the part they were playing in relation to the reorganization of secondary education.

One chief education officer in a borough where a system of groups has been introduced thought that Heads who previously had had their own governing body were dissatisfied with the present system, with its larger meetings and undignified queuing outside the committee room, but those who had not experienced the luxury of their own governing body did not seem to mind greatly. Most of the difficulties were raised by Heads who had had no previous experience of grouping; but now the system was being accepted.

This borough advertised for nominations to its governing bodies to be made both by 'reputable bodies' and individuals, but the arrangements were entirely in the hands of the Town Clerk, and the chief education officer was unable to supply much information about the number of nominations received or the selection procedure followed.

Previously a head had been appointed by a procedure which involved members of the Council and the *whole* governing body.

Now there was what amounted virtually to a staffing sub-committee composed of six members of the Council and six members of the governing body. Shortlisting for the post was performed by the whole governing body, advised by a professional officer.

The status of governing bodies in this authority is illustrated by the progress of the local plan for secondary reorganization, which was prepared by a working party consisting of members of the Education Committee, teacher representatives, and professional officers. The scheme was presented to the Education Committee, and after approval was communicated to the governing bodies. It was then the subject of various public meetings. Throughout the governors were kept 'well-informed', and although they did not influence the basis of the scheme they did raise detailed questions relating to its implementation. In all, the scheme was not substantially modified by either the public or the governors. The plan had been criticized in some local circles as a 'botched-up scheme', but the Department of Education and Science, which undertook a thorough examination of it in the lights of its opponents' criticisms, had not been able to suggest an alternative. This example clearly corroborates R. H. Pear's view, in his foreword to *Policies and Politics in Secondary Education*, by D. Peschek and J. A. Brand, 1966 (p. 5), that 'politicians, planners and pressure groups are of scant importance if the existing bricks and mortar of old schools are located in the "wrong" places.'

In a second borough it was reported that teachers found it difficult to see what governors did, as they were still only 'platform figures'. In this authority, however, it is only fair to say that the authority was largely marking time until secondary reorganization, based on the middle school pattern, had been completed. Then it was intended to have one governing body, consisting of not more than twelve members, representing the schools in each tier of the pyramid. This amounted to a reduced version of the former system.

In another borough one of the constituent elements had fought a rearguard action against the establishment of individual governing bodies, arguing that they lived in a tightly-knit community, and all the governors could do could be handled by a sub-committee. When the borough was formed, an attempt was made to bring this element into line with the rest, and for eighteen months a management sub-committee existed to look after secondary schools. When secondary reorganization became effective in late 1967, eleven new comprehensive schools (two of them voluntary controlled schools), each with its own governing body, had been established.

It is interesting to note that when the governing bodies of the new schools were to be recast there was an announcement in the local papers. Many people then wrote to the chief education officer saying that they would like to serve; but this met with no response from the authority and the political balance of the council was again reflected on the governing bodies. Furthermore, the chief education officer doubted the advantage of having governing bodies assist in the appointment of teaching staff and also the extent to which governing bodies could serve as a link with the public. He conceded that in a larger authority where the administration was more impersonal a governing body might be of some use, but although the new borough was considerably larger than its former elements it was not so large as to warrant the creation of a separate system of governing bodies. He thus subscribed to the common fallacy which equates size in an authority with an impersonal style of administration.

In so far as conclusions can be drawn from these follow-up studies they are that there had been up to the time of the second study no substantial re-thinking of existing practices. Only where a borough had been formed from constituent elements with divergent approaches to school government had changes resulted.

TWO EXPERIMENTS

The two other studies of school government in transition deal with county boroughs in the North and the Midlands. The first is of a county borough which had introduced individual governing bodies for its comprehensive schools. In the other county borough special meetings had been arranged for the discussion of general educational topics. This had been envisaged as a means of injecting fresh life into the proceedings of governing bodies which were concerned with a number of new schools.

In the first authority the chief education officer said that one argument he had had to meet against the introduction of individual governing bodies was that it would mean extra expense and the appointment of additional staff. This had not been the case as the costs were met by unpaid overtime: administrative officers and inspectors took it in turn to attend governors' meetings, and regarded this as being all in the day's (or the evening's) work. The composition of governing bodies had been recast. Under the previous system the majority of the members were councillors, but there were now no more than three in each governing body, with the chairmanship and vice-chairmanship going to members of different parties. Politics did not really enter into governors' meetings. Some of the councillors on the governing bodies were not on the Education Committee, and this was thought valuable, as they saw something of the workings of a service other than their main interest. One head said that the recruitment of outsiders had resulted in the appointment of such people as a local vicar, a university representative, a farmer's wife, an apprentice supervisor, a foreman and a welfare worker. Among these were two parents and two candidates nominated by the head. With this kind of balance, the head argued, the governors could take an all-round view, and could each contribute some specialist knowledge of the area, of local employment or of some aspect of education. The governors could take the initiative and ensure that the Education Committee considered and possibly approved their requests; they had supported his proposal for the appointment of a full-time technician for crafts and visual aids, and even though this was turned down on administrative grounds, they had pressed their claim further. As a result the Education Committee was considering the principles that should underly such appointments. Such intervention on major issues was relatively uncommon. However, on occasion the authority had been known to reverse administrative decisions, particularly if it could be shown via the governors that officers were obtuse or obstructive. Major decisions were made in committee rather than by officers, and the governors had a role to play in ensuring that matters were brought to the Committee's attention.

Local people often went to governors for advice and with complaints. These were almost invariably referred to the head and he was thus able to see how his decisions looked from the other side. Parents, he felt, were often more afraid to approach the head than a governor. There was still a feeling among some sectors of the community that the head was a person who simply could not be challenged.

Another head in this authority did not view the new system so highly. He accepted that his governing body was three times as useful as its predecessor, if only because it met three times as often. In addition, the presence of a body that was prepared to advocate the needs of *one* school was an encouragement to a head who was tired of fighting on his own *ad nauseam* and *ad infinitum*. Even so, this head dismissed his governors as weak, unintelligent, ineffective and generally useless. They did not visit the school and he never saw them save at meetings (the interviewer thought that he might have driven some of them away by his manner and by making them too aware of his low opinion of them). They functioned as a pressure group as far as getting money was concerned, but they were not very good at that.

A third head expressed a very different view. He had found that his governors were interested in visiting the school and on their own initiative had come to lunch with staff and boys. Some were useful as links with the local community, and some people, such as vicars and doctors, were in a strategic position, as they heard all the local gossip. Such people were shrewd, articulate and in touch with local feeling. The additional interest which governors showed in the school as a result of the new system was very welcome, even if some had bees in their bonnets. Under the old system governors meetings were poorly attended: now it was a matter of personal honour to attend meetings and functions, and attendance was very good indeed. He felt that both he and the school had been given a tremendous psychological boost. More specifically, governors with industrial or professional interests could help to bridge the gap between school and work. Teachers as a body knew little about industry and people in industry little about schools. An example of this could be seen in their differing attitudes to the CSE, which industrialists tended to regard as something very much like GCE, setting great store by a certain number of passes at a certain level, whereas teachers emphasized the need to adapt the examination to the requirements of the individual child, and to base the syllabus largely on the school's own ideas and less on some pattern predetermined outside the school.

This follow-up study was illuminating, as it produced three heads who each had a very different outlook on governing bodies and the local education authority. One expressed himself as being in favour of strengthening links between the school and the community via the governors; another had little time for them; and the views of the third consisted of the 'conventional wisdom' of heads. All had been at their schools for some years and favoured the change in varying degrees.

The picture presented by the second study is less sanguine, showing how good intentions can lead to insignificant results. The authority concerned had decided to have two meetings of governing bodies each year, one in the autumn term being concerned with administrative matters, and the other in the spring term being devoted to educational topics. The secondary school system operating at the time included junior high schools for the 11–13 age group, and senior schools from 13–16 or 13–18, with two 11–19 schools on the outskirts of the authority's area. The bulk of places on these governing bodies were filled by councillors and they had very few powers devolved upon them. Administratively they were considered as impotent and a waste of time for both heads and councillors.

The two aims of the spring term meeting were said to be the

education of the governors, and the provision of a link between different tiers of the comprehensive system. Early fears by heads that attendance would be poor proved to be groundless, as at both meetings it was approximately 90 per cent, but their suspicion that there would be very little discussion proved to be justified. No councillor, apart from the chairman, spoke at either meeting. Discussion on curriculum reform was initiated by a teacher representative who criticized the lack of use made of a curriculum development centre which had just been opened. This brought a sharp rebuff from the chief education officer, who hastened to inform the meeting that the centre was busy every night of the week. Later a head argued that difficulties in coordination were aggravated by the breakdown of the zoning scheme in use, and asked whether it could be more strictly enforced. This led to the chairman of the education committee making a short speech on the impracticability of this being done and on the freedom of parents to have some choice as regards the schools their children attended.

This situation is in marked contrast to that resulting from the other experiment described, where stress had been laid on the individuality of each school and its governing body. In this second case the new procedure was too similar to the existing arrangements for most participants to be aware of any change of role. In particular, the heads were uncertain what was expected of them, and the parent representatives felt depressed and subordinate. The majority of those present were hard-pressed councillors and, in these circumstances, it was not likely that any fresh opportunities for educational discussion would be exploited. Any suggestion brought forward at such a meeting, moreover, could be held to be a potential threat to officers or heads, since it might be interpreted as a criticism of them for having failed to take necessary action. All in all, the experiment seems to illustrate the difficulty of developing an effective forum for discussion and the free exchange of information and advice within a committee structure essentially executive in nature.

THE GOVERNMENT OF BOARDING SCHOOLS MAINTAINED BY LOCAL EDUCATION AUTHORITIES

The existence of a small number of schools maintained by local education authorities is of particular interest for students of school government, in so far as they throw light on the relative importance of the kind of control a local authority exercises and the kind of control appropriate for school which is a residential institution. Discussions were held with heads of such schools and with the officers of local education authorities responsible for them. The schools concerned were both selective and non-selective. Particular attention was paid to the selection of pupils, the appointment of staff and powers of local purchase.

The procedure operating in one authority illustrates the extent of a head's freedom to select or reject pupils. Application forms, after completion by parents, were scrutinized by the heads and administrative officers at County Hall. Priority was given to those whose background made boarding especially desirable or essential (i.e. on the principles enumerated in the Martin Report of 1960). One of the heads had to agree to accept a priority case, or else give an extremely good reason for his refusal. If no head was willing, the authority undertook to find a place elsewhere. Applications from non-priority candidates were considered in the light of a recommendation from the applicant's primary school head. The main criterion used was that of ability to benefit from boarding education, specified by some heads as the possession of self-reliance and the ability to make a positive contribution to the life of the school. All applicants, priority and non-priority, were interviewed with at least one of their parents, with the heads sitting as a panel. This procedure, although exhausting, enabled the heads to rebut charges of unfair rejection which might be made by disgruntled parents or by councillors acting on their behalf. It was thought that all suitable applicants were offered a place at one of the authority's schools or at some other schools where the authority took up places. Where heads thought that applicants were obviously unsuitable for a normal boarding school (e.g. pupils who showed signs of being completely disruptive, who were chronic bed-wetters or who required some form of special treatment), they could persuade the authority to place them elsewhere.

In another authority it was confirmed that there was a lot of give and take between the authority and boarding school heads over admissions. The authority attached great importance to the head's own assessment, since the type of pupil who might be quite acceptable, or at least tolerable, in a day school could easily be out of place in a more closed boarding community. In this authority heads would visit the applicant's primary school, talk to the boy and his own head and see his work. As in the other authority, they would obtain their governors' formal confirmation of proposed offers and rejections, in order to avoid any outcry from disappointed parents. All the heads interviewed confirmed that they were rarely pressed to take pupils whom they did not consider at all suitable, and that to a very great extent they had the last word. They were aware of their obligations to take priority cases, but even in this sphere the shortage of places in relation to the demand gave them a very considerable degree of discretion.

In sociological terms a boarding school is much more of a 'total community' than is a day school; and it naturally follows that the person in day to day charge will appear to have more absolute control simply because his interest is not confined to the normal working hours of a day school. The school regime is more complex and wide-reaching, and extends over many dimensions which are simply not met with in day schools. In considering such matters as the organization and management of boarding houses, the appointment of non-teaching staff, extra-curricular activities, the control of pupils outside teaching hours and the general responsibility of heads to act *in loco parentis*, it becomes apparent that any such heads must be left to make his own decisions. Moreover, most local authority boarding schools are run by counties, and counties generally have a rather looser system of administration, with a greater delegation to individual institutions, than boroughs. Where a school does not serve a definable neighbour-hood interest, and particularly where it is situated outside the territory of its parent authority, detailed control and supervision by the authority is even less likely. Also, since the provision of boarding schools by local authorities is still at a relatively un-developed stage, such schools are regarded as something of a novelty requiring an experimental approach. Heads in such schools, for example, appear to have a very free hand in the appointment of teaching and non-teaching staff, being able to take into account their personal suitability for life in a boarding estab-lishment, as well as their formal qualifications and professional experience. It seems rare that the governing body of a maintained boarding school take a close interest in the appointment of assistant teachers, but even where they do they invariably pay great attention to the head's views.

It is often found convenient to make special arrangements for boarding schools in such matters as local purchase and supplies of materials and for minor repairs and improvements. Even though heads appreciate getting a substantial discount through their county supplies officer, running a boarding school is so complex an operation that it is generally much more convenient to get as many matters as possible seen to locally. The force of this argu-ment is admitted by local education authority officers, and by members of governing bodies.

Governors, indeed, whilst taking a very close interest in their schools, are prepared to give their heads a considerable amount of freedom. They do not appear to challenge their decisions on such matters as the amount of visiting by parents that is permitted, the organization of extra-curricular activities, or in-school or out-of-school discipline. In many respects indeed, the relationships of heads and governors resemble those typical of the independent sector, rather than those generally found in maintained day schools.

5 The Functions of Governing Bodies

THE APPOINTMENT OF TEACHING STAFF

HEADS

In all local education authorities, except county boroughs without governing bodies, governors are involved in some way in the appointment of the head of the school, and this is regarded as one of their most important functions. Practices adopted closely follow the procedures laid down in the Model Articles of government. These have already been described and there is relatively little to add to the discussion in Chapter 3 of the reasons given for following one procedure rather than another. There was generally satisfaction with whichever procedure was used save in a few cases in which governors felt that they played a subordinate role. In one area studied it was suggested that where a joint committee is weighted to the advantage of the authority, the interest of the governors diminishes and they consequently fail sometimes to turn up. Where the alternative procedure is followed, and governors meet separately for the first stage of the appointing process, they are said to resent it if the authority subsequently does not accept their first choice. This, it is said, can result in a new head receiving a somewhat cool reception from the governors later.

Control of the short-list is, of course, of great importance. The extent to which this control modifies the role of the governing body can be seen from an examination of the procedure for appointing a head in a typical authority with governing bodies for individual schools or groups of schools. Advertisements are placed in the national educational press and notification of the appointment sent to all local schools and colleges. Applications are received in the education office where the chief education officer in person or his senior professional colleagues—or both together—sort them roughly into impossibles, possibles, and probables, for interview purposes. References are taken up for the probables and, depending on the number and quality of applicants, for the possibles as well. Discreet enquiries may be made through the professional old-boy network about the probables. The full list will be seen in most cases by the chairman of governors and his deputy, who will approve the short-list, or present it to the full governing body for their approval before applicants are called for interview by the joint committee. It is at this point that the laymen may take an active part by discussing the presence or absence of certain names on the short-list, even though it may be generally held that it is the responsibility of the professional officers on their own to select a sufficient and varied list of suitably qualified and experienced candidates for consideration. A chairman might, for example, suggest that X who is not on the short-list seems no worse on paper than Y who is, or that another woman candidate, or another applicant from within the authority, should be included. Chief education officers may sometimes suspect that a layman may be urging the claims of an acquaintance or a party supporter, and a number have mentioned how distasteful they found it to put candidates on short-lists with the intention of not seeing them appointed. They are generally confident that special pleading will prove unavailing when such candidates are compared with others at interview, although it would appear from some reports that canvassing and favouritism are, in certain areas, not entirely dead yet. In the great majority of cases, however, the short-list goes through unchallenged and most chief education officers consider that it constitutes an adequate safeguard. Many affirm that it is by virtue of their control of the short-list that they are able to acquiesce in their committee's or their governors' free hand in the final selection. As a result they are relatively unconcerned with the formal procedure for interviewing applicants, although in some county boroughs they shrank out of shame when interviews were held by the full education committee. One chief education officer was convinced that many first-class candidates turned down invitations after such an experience; but, as a man of great tact, this was one point he claimed he could not make to his good friend the chairman!

To sum up, the first general principle observed in the appointment of heads is that it is for professional administrators to ensure that proper weight is given to qualifications and experience. This principle is embodied in the practice of allowing the chief education officer a virtually free hand in short-listing. The second general principle is that the screened candidates should be judged by laymen for those qualities of personality and suitability for the school and the area which any experienced body of 'good men and true' should be able to discern. This principle is embodied in selection by governing bodies, joint committees or the education committee itself. Chief education officers feel quite happy with any system as long as they have security in drawing up the short-list. Difficulties arise when laymen are thought to be interfering in this, or when there is a severe shortage of acceptable applicants. Only in one or two cases did chief education officers admit that the appointment of heads was quite beyond professional control. In one authority a selection committee was very suspicous of the officers and insisted on sifting all applications themselves. By the time they had considered some seventy, spread over two meetings, they were more than ready to hand things over to the local inspector and the divisional officer. Selection controlled by a group of laymen might produce a bias, sometimes quite deliberate, in favour of local candidates. This implies a narrowness of outlook that can be condemned; but in an area where local feeling is strong, an intimate understanding of the forms it takes is almost a necessary qualification for the head of a school, and the appointment of an outsider could court disaster. Finally, when governors have taken an active, possibly decisive, part in the appointment of 'their' head, they can more confidently introduce him to the locality and help him to settle down and gain acceptance. However outlandish his ideas, and however 'foreign' the man himself, he cannot be a complete stranger to the community if the governors are known to be involved and—in part, at least—responsible for his appointment.

ASSISTANT TEACHING STAFF

The Counties

It has been seen that the model articles afford the local education authority the utmost elasticity in the appointment of assistant teaching staff, and the extent to which governors participate varies from authority to authority and from school to school. On the whole, the counties favour dispersal of control and the part governors are able to play can be substantial; the county boroughs prefer closer control of schools by the education office, and the power to appoint staff lies with the head and the office.

The variety of practice found in the counties can be described briefly. In only five was it general practice for heads to appoint staff without consulting their governors, and in two cases this was provided for in the articles of government. In a number of authorities the head might make all appointments on his own except for the most senior, on which he would consult his chairman of governors. In some authorities all governors would be invited to appointments meetings, although it was not considered essential for all to turn up. In others, the head might appoint with his chairman of governors; or there might be an appointments sub-committee; or the full governing body might participate.

How far governors take part in the appointment of staff depends very much on the place they are accorded in the administrative system, and on the degree of confidence which exists between the education office, the head and themselves. For junior staff it is quite normal for heads to make appointments, although some governors feel happier if the chairman at least is brought in. This is generally regarded as a highly satisfactory arrangement, since it gives heads considerable independence of action, but a second opinion can be called upon when necessary. The involvement of governors is considered desirable for senior posts, and it is interesting to note that, in the two authorities where heads have the right to make all appointments, some still prefer to involve their governors. Many chief education officers found it difficult to come down either in favour of or against governors' participation, or to specify the nature of the contribution they might make. They tended to take refuge in that oldest of generalities, 'It all depends on personalities'.

In reply to the HMM questionnaire, 70 per cent of the 132 heads in the counties revealed that their governors—the chairman, a sub-committee or the full body—took part in staff appointments. 52 per cent of this group of heads found lay participation helpful, 26 per cent did not mind their governors' presence (although the heads themselves were always left to make the decision), while 22 per cent stated that the governors were useless or obstructive. The general effectiveness of governors' participation is thought to be least when the full body is involved. Governors can be shrewd assessors of personality even if they cannot judge professional qualifications. They can ask general questions about candidates' attitudes and experience; and a second opinion is always useful, especially for senior appointments. A few heads found it useful to share the responsibility of making appointments in case they did not turn out well; and when personal factors made a decision difficult, for example, when a member of staff was applying for promotion within a school, the responsibility for negative decision can be passed to the governors. Arguments against the involvement of governors are that they can make no useful contribution in what is essentially a professional matter, that they sometimes seek to impose their own views and that, more specifically, their participation can cause delay which is intolerable at a time of staff shortage.

Of the 190 university governors in county authorities studied 76 took part in the appointment of staff. But in some authorities it was assumed that appointments were the prerogative of the authority's representatives and university governors were deliberately kept off appointments sub-committees. This practice was greatly resented as university governors felt themselves to be excluded from the one function where they might make their most valuable contribution. The arguments used by those who did take part in appointing staff were similar to those advanced by heads who favoured governors' participation. Governors were of use even though the final decision rested almost invariably with the head; the questioning of candidates by the governors and subsequent discussion were thought to have some bearing on the head's decision, and might reveal facets of personality which would have otherwise gone unnoticed. One or two university governors mentioned that heads' judgments and preferences were not infallible and that occasionally, when they were very sure of their ground, governors would be justified in overruling a head's expressed choice. One or two heads admitted that when this had happened to them, the governors had been right in restrospect. Less extreme examples of governors' interventions occur when they persuade a head not to fill a post immediately from a few applicants of low calibre, but to wait a time until the field is better. One head who had accepted his governors' arguments agreed that their intervention was justified, as it was easy to make a bad appointment but much more difficult to get rid of an unsatisfactory teacher.

The advantages of governors' participation were also stressed in our area studies of county authorities, and of the Inner London Education Authority. The general weight of opinion among those interviewed was in favour of the involvement of governors, especially for important posts. Governors might feel all at sea when it came to details of finance, but they thought they were capable of judging between one person and another, and were willing to accept professional advice on professional qualifications.

The County Boroughs

The compactness of county boroughs allows more contact between individual schools and the education office, and governors' involvement in the appointment of staff may be very slight indeed. They are rarely concerned with the appointment of newly qualified teachers, who are generally recruited *en bloc* to the service of the authority and then appointed or assigned to individual schools.

Lay appointment of assistants, in a time of perpetual shortage of teachers has become, except in a handful of fortunate authorities, an anachronism. There is also a trend against lay involvement in appointments to senior posts. In authorities where a sub-committee acts as a governing body or the governing body deals with a large number of schools, these appointments are often left to professional officers. Many graded posts are filled, on the recommendation of the head, by teachers promoted from within the school, and at a fairly junior level it would be unlikely for the officers, let alone a governing body, to contest the head's recommendations. Heads are also in a powerful position as regards head of department posts even when formal procedures put the selection and final appointment in the hands of others. The degree of influence a head can exert depends on how far he carries weight with staff at the education office and with his governors, and on the amount of confidence they have in him. In no county borough is the head expressly excluded from consideration in the appointment of heads of department, although the office may see fit to overrule his request for the promotion of a particular teacher. The formal procedure for appointments to senior posts is often invoked only when the head does not wish to recommend a member of his staff for promotion. If there is doubt over a head's recommendation, the chief education officer might advise that the teacher concerned be put to the test of open competition and selection. In these circumstances governors are clearly able to play a positive part.

In the appointment of deputy heads governors play a larger part than for junior staff and heads of departments. In 31 county boroughs with governing bodies the governors select the deputy head, and in 16 more selection is by chairman of governors, the head and professional officers. In only 10 such authorities is the appointment of deputy heads left to an appointments sub-committee of the education committee, whilst only one authority leaves it to its professional staff. This least practice also operates in 3 authorities without governing bodies. In comparison with the procedure for the appointment of heads of department, governors are afforded a much more substantial role, while at the same time the head is also given a large say. He will almost certainly consider the applicants with the professional officers and help to draw up a short list with his chairman of governors and a senior officer; he will normally see the candidates and show them round the school before the formal interviews; and, however the latter are conducted, the governors or the appointing sub-committee will be unlikely to force on the head someone he does not want. In only 2 authorities were heads deliberately excluded from having a say in the appointment of their deputies. In the one case they were kept out by politicians jealous of their prerogatives, and in the other they were kept out because the committee felt that in the past their assessments had not been sufficiently objective and hence had been misleading.

How far did heads in county boroughs find it desirable for their governors to be involved in staff appointments? Questionnaires received from 76 heads in county boroughs showed that governors were involved in only 45 per cent of the schools, in many of these only in respect of more senior appointments. Where governors were involved 56 per cent of the heads found them helpful, 19 per cent said they left the decision to the head although they might attend the interviewing meeting, and 25 per cent found their governors useless or obstructive. 23 heads in county boroughs where there is no governing body system in any real sense were asked how they thought they might benefit from having governors to assist them with teaching appointments. 20 members of this group did not think they would benefit at all: it would detract from their independence and cause delay. The three others who thought they might benefit were divided between two who considered it useful to discuss appointments with a body of people who know the head and the school, and one who thought that to have a governing body to consult over staff appointments might be quicker than the present system of appointing staff through administrative channels only.

Evidence from area studies in county boroughs confirmed that the involvement of governors was not very great except in senior posts. One county borough visited did not bring governors into the appointing procedure at all, and appointments were made by a staffing sub-committee. This system was approved of by the education committee and by heads except when it caused delay. All other county boroughs studied involved governors to some extent, in that at least the chairman was concerned with the more senior posts to be filled. It was left to the head, possibly with an administrative officer, to appoint junior staff. Heads generally seemed satisfied with these arrangements save that they did not like mass appointments of new teachers by the authority. This often meant that heads had little say as to whom of those so appointed should be assigned to their schools. Amongst governors the usual view taken was that for senior appointments a layman should be involved in addition to the head, but that since it was the latter who had to work with the person appointed he should have a substantial say. This view was supported by university governors who stressed that, with the increasing complexities of school organization, heads may feel a need for support in the making of difficult decisions.

In some local education authorities there is a marked difference in practice between selective and non-selective schools. The replies to the NSH Questionnaire showed that in the counties only some 27 out of 119 heads claimed to appoint their senior staff themselves and in the county boroughs this was only occasionally the case.

Very substantial evidence emerged both from comments attracted by the questionnaire surveys and by the detailed area studies to show the need for governors to have relevant and varied collective experience to offer, whether this has been gained from public life, from man-management or from a general knowledge of education or young people. In addition, guidance is essential for those joining a governing body for the first time. A few authorities issue handbooks to governors which include sections on interviewing. Advice on how not to do it though may be more valuable than positive suggestions, if embarrassment is not to be caused through the asking of such questions as 'Do you drink?', 'Do you like children?' and 'What is your philosophy of life?' It is true that tactful advice on the spot from an inspector or the head can concentrate governors' questions on appropriate matters. However, such informal guidance has to be unobtrusive; there are accounts of appalling results when independent (or bloody-minded) governors have resented any guidance, even couched in the most general terms, and have refused to appoint the candidate apparently favoured by the head. In one authority an over-emphasis on detailed guidance produced a procedure of a very bizarre kind. For assistant staff appointments the whole governing body met, having taken an active share in the preparation of the short-list. Before the meeting, the governors agreed on three questions to be put in turn, with no other questions permitted. When all candidates had been seen, the governors proceeded to a vote without further discussion. At no stage was the head asked for, or permitted to express, his views. Such a practice cannot conceivably be in the interests of any of the parties concerned. It is quite astonishing that it persists and is accepted in any local education authority.

GOVERNING BODIES AND FINANCE

A potentially important function formally assigned to governing bodies in articles of government is the presentation of estimates to the local education authority. In practice governors' involvement in this task is very small and does not generally go beyond rubber-stamping estimates drawn up by the authority's staff on their own or in consultation with the head of the school.

According to the chief education officers, in four out of every five authorities governors' concern with drawing up annual estimates was purely nominal. Indeed, 4 counties and 5 county boroughs, all but one of which had governing bodies for groups of schools (or one governing body for all secondary schools), had dispensed with estimates for individual schools. A further 3 county boroughs (2 with small grouped bodies) kept separate estimates for selective schools only. In the remaining one out of five authorities it was felt that governors did have a part to play;

they were given an opportunity to scrutinize the estimates closely, to put forward their own suggestions, to exclude some items, and to draw up a list of priorities. However, even in these authorities the revised estimates would be altered subsequently by the education committee, and reference back to the governing body was seldom considered necessary.

EVIDENCE FROM AREA STUDIES

A lack of financial responsibility was confirmed in the area studies. While in some areas governors were accorded an administrative and advisory role in financial matters, the authority's general overriding responsibility made this role very subordinate. In 5 of the 6 county boroughs which were studied in depth governors played no part at all, or only a nominal part, in preparing estimates. Liability to subsequent cuts made their submission a pointless exercise, although it might make councillors who were also governors more sympathetic to the claims of the schools. Governors might make special recommendations, or help by an initial review of their heads' requests; even so, this procedure was thought to contain an element of ritual, and was by no means regarded as an essential administrative process. In one authority the governors controlled a £50 contingency fund, to be spent on items which the 'office' did not provide. This 'power' was looked on by the heads as a sop to the governors; one head pointed out that the sum amounted to less than 2 per cent of the total expenditure, and was spent on trivial items which in most authorities he would have been able to spend on his own. In another authority the capitation allowance was left to the head to spend, but governors' approval had to be obtained for items over £100—but this was normally a formality.

Only in one county borough did governors play more than a subsidiary role. This can be explained by the peculiar financial arrangements obtaining in this authority. In the financial allocation to schools there was no element of capitation, and all requests for current expenditure by heads had to pass through the governing body, chiefly through the annual estimates which were discussed and approved by the governors before being submitted to the education committee. In interviews with heads it became clear that they genuinely thought that their governors exercised real power in agreeing to or refusing their requests. The estimates meeting was a test of their ability to justify their proposals, and that the governors submitted the latter to searching examination. They also felt that once this had been done, they were safe. Even if the governors' estimates meeting could not be the ultimate control, it was an effective and respected stage in the total process. However, in many ways this authority can be considered as exceptional because of the absence of a capitation system at a time when elsewhere these systems were becoming more comprehensive. It is also significant that its governing bodies included people who held the respect of the officers with whom they dealt, and who were not content to accept a head's claim without query; and finally there was a deliberate policy of giving governors a defined role in this aspect of educational administration.

Of the county authorities studied, only one took the part played by governors in drawing up estimates seriously; and two examples from the others illustrate their financial impotence. In one wholly divisional county governors were required to submit the estimates to the local education authority in November. However, since the divisional executive was required to submit all its estimates to the authority in October, the governors' submission was purely a formality. Moreover, even when the governors saw the estimates, they were presented in such a form that it was impossible for the uninitiated to know what they meant. In practice the headmaster made out his estimates and passed them to the divisional officer who went through them before submitting them to the authority. The latter allocated global sums to each division, leaving it to the divisional officers to work out their priorities. In another county a very great degree of freedom in the financial running of the schools had devolved on the heads, to the almost complete exclusion of the governing bodies. Each school had a bank account into which the entire school allowance was paid. Although heads were advised to consult with their governing bodies on the allocation of the school's resources, this meant no more than getting their formal approval, normally through the chairman of governors.

In the one county in which governors' consideration of the estimates was taken seriously an extra meeting of each governing body was held in the autumn term. At this the draft estimates, drawn up by the head in consultation with the 'office' were considered, with the help of a senior administrative officer. Governors were able to discuss proposals fully, to insert and delete items, and to make positive suggestions. As in other authorities, estimates so carefully considered might be later cut back, but it was not considered a waste of time for the governors to go through them in draft. They were looked on as people on the spot who knew the needs of the schools, and their recommendations carried weight.

Time is one of the factors which militates against governors' playing an active part in the preparation of estimates, particularly in counties with systems of divisional administration. In order to be considered by all the committees concerned, estimates have to be submitted to governors up to nine months before consideration of the authority's overall budget. Indeed, reference has already been made to an even more absurd situation. Estimates might therefore either be out of date by the time they were finally approved, or else be couched in such general terms as to give no guarantee that money voted would be spent on items specifically requested.

Apart from the time factor, the automatic nature of much local education authority expenditure on education makes it difficult for a body of governors to play a constructive part. By far the greatest proportion of the money spent on schools, for example the salaries of teachers, major maintenance and repair work, heating and lighting and related expenditure, is beyond the power of the governors—or even the authority itself—to control.[1] A very large proportion of a school's annual expenditure is necessarily determined before the governors can possibly have a say.

[1] Cf. Birley, D., *The Education Officer and his World*, 1970, pp. 30-1.

Governors' lack of real powers in respect of school finance was stressed in replies to the questionnaires addressed to university governors. About two-thirds of the respondents who served in county authorities, and about three-quarters in county boroughs, felt that governors did not influence the allocation of financial resources. Where governors were said to have some influence, it was through the discussion of heads' proposals, and through pressure which might be exerted on the authority by a resolution of the governors. Two positive suggestions were made for increasing governors' financial powers. The first was a block grant system, on a capitation basis, for everything except building works, with money deposited in the school bank, administered by the governors and subject to audit, with all allocations made by the governors. Another university governor thought that the Department of Education and Science and local education authorities should insist only on minima and should be directly responsible for the provision of resources to enable these minima to be met: the governing body would then be allocated resources for provision above and beyond the minima so that schools could evolve their own highly individual sets of characteristics.

The first proposal is an extension of practices already found in some authorities, where each school has its own bank account and where the head has a greater or less degree of freedom to spend the school allowance as he thinks fit. From interviews with heads in one of these authorities it did not appear that governors were any more deeply involved with their schools' detailed expenditure; approval for the purchase of quite large items is regarded as a pure formality. The second proposal is unlikely to find favour with authorities concerned with developing a coherent system of education, offering a full range of courses in their area, rather than with promoting self-sufficient schools which might be bidding against each other for scarce resources or not providing adequately between them for certain needs, particularly those apparent over a wider area than that served by any one school.

In the Inner London Education Authority governors might authorize the spending of sums of up to £25 on repairs and £50 on minor improvements. They also approved estimates and recommended the supply of special equipment or the award of additional allowances. It was generally agreed by those interviewed that the governors' financial powers were purely formal. The initiative for expenditure on repairs and minor improvements invariably came from the heads and governors regarded the approval of the estimates as merely 'rubber-stamping'. At the most, it could be claimed only that governors are kept fully informed of the schools' financial position. There was a general acceptance that, in a highly centralized authority where furniture, equipment and materials were obtained through systems of bulk purchase via the Supplies Department, there was relatively little scope for schools to have greater financial autonomy. Occasionally heads complained that they could not go round the corner and get a local man to do a little job, and that their powers of local purchase were too restricted. But, in fact, heads had powers to spend a proportion of their combined allowance (generally 10 per cent) by local purchase, and could spend up to £10 on minor repairs without reference to their governors. Some heads were reluctant to use these powers, preferring to call on the authority's services.

It is not clear how governors would benefit from any greater devolution of financial powers, as compared with heads or divisional officers, who have quite substantial powers over the authorization of minor works. Divisional officers could, for example, at the time of the enquiry, approve projects costing up to £1,500; and this considerable discretion enjoyed by administrative officers is sometimes contrasted with the £50 limit set for the representatives of the community, the governors. But it is the governors who have to take the initiative in asking for minor works to be carried out, or for extra allowances to the authorized. Divisional officers may have as many as 150 schools to cope with and since there is a chronic shortage of money, they necessarily confine their attention to requests received. Both for matters which can be settled locally and for those which must be referred to County Hall, the point of play is necessarily at the Divisional Office. This situation can lead to some feelings of frustration among governors, who feel that they carry no weight with the authority as such. However, more than half of the university governors consulted felt they did influence final allocations to their schools, and that they caused the authority to have second thoughts even though these second thoughts might be restricted to minor matters.

It can be said, and without qualification, that governors' financial powers are negligible, and that there is no prospect of any significant increase. This is borne out by their lack of power to take decisions about the contingency allowances to which reference has been made. Most authorities and teachers would probably regard the absence of a capitation system as far too high a price to pay for the active involvement of governing bodies in financial matters. The time factors, especially in two-tier counties, the increase in the administrative discretion granted to officers and heads, the provision by the authorities of services for supplies, repairs and maintenance, and above all the automatic nature of the bulk of school expenditure, all combine to leave governing bodies a role of no executive importance. They can make themselves fully informed of the school's financial position, and find out where the money goes. It has been shown that this function was taken seriously in two authorities and the communication of information was felt to involve the governors intimately in the affairs of the school. They may still have been a rubber-stamp, but a rubber-stamp with a difference. However, taking the initiative is seen as a valuable function for active governors. But to be informed and to be able to initiate are not the same as to have power to take decisions and allocate resources, and many would argue that they are an inadequate substitute. But they cannot be dismissed entirely.

THE CURRICULUM[2]

Few, if any, functions of governing bodies produce so many stock reactions as their 'general oversight of the school and its curri-

[2] This discussion of the relationships between governors, heads and authorities in relation to the curriculum—and the others which follow in relation to disci-

culum'. Time after time heads claimed that they were entirely responsible for deciding what was to be taught, but that they might report major changes to their governors as matters of information. Similarly, one governor after another said that he would never dream of interfering with the curriculum, and that it is all left to the head. A number of factors combine to inhibit the great majority of governors from taking any close interest in curricular matters. There is the standard clause in the articles of government establishing the head's responsibility for the internal organization and discipline of the school; there is the long-standing tradition that the content of education should be left to the teachers, with the associated view that the head as a responsible professional should be left to get on with the job; there is a feeling that laymen are not competent to raise educational issues themselves, and a reluctance to challenge the head on his own ground; and there is a general desire to avoid demarcation disputes over the respective responsibilities of heads and governors.

The net result is that in very many cases governors take only a perfunctory interest in the curriculum, merely noting what the head chooses to tell them. This is exactly what is wanted by many heads, as they feel their governors are not competent to express an opinion. Governors' influence on the curriculum was thought to be minimal, to judge from the heads' and university governors' replies in the questionnaire surveys, while chief education officers confirmed that instances of unwelcome interest or intervention by governors were few and far between. Indeed, the view was sometimes expressed by heads that governors could well take a greater interest without invading the professional domain. The standard clauses in articles of government are so generally worded as to force both heads and governors on the defensive: the 'con-

plinary issues and the ways in which governors may keep in touch with their schools—are based on nearly three hundred interviews conducted in the course of the 'area studies' of some three hundred authorities. In this aspect of the study the general interviews carried out in all authorities and the questionnaire surveys could not give major help: what was necessary was close contact with heads in their schools, with members of their governing bodies and with those administrative officers who knew the affairs of the schools concerned.

duct and curriculum' of the school is the concern of the governors, but its 'organization, management and discipline' is a matter for the head (with the local education authority having an overriding responsibility on both counts).

It would be reasonable to expect that any body charged with a general interest in the work of a school should regard what is taught as one of its most important and rewarding concerns. Active interest in the curriculum need not diminish the head's own responsibility or make him feel that he is necessarily accountable to his governors, although many heads are under this impression: nor need it be limited to receiving a formal report from the head at meetings of the governing body. It can manifest itself through governors taking part in the appointment of staff, where they can learn something of the head's expectations and the experience and approaches to teaching of new members of staff; it can also be developed through informal visits to see the school at work and to talk to the staff. Heads welcome this sort of involvement in the life of the school and do not regard it as detracting from their professional dignity; but when it comes to discussing examination results or the introduction of new subjects, they tend to be much more guarded in their approval, being willing to give their governors only a general picture, and discouraging questions.

Governing bodies are most co-operative when the head regards them and their opinions as worthy of respect, and when he is ready to communicate his problems to them. Without initiative from the head a governing body can do little to become an effective partner. Such considerations apply to governors' involvement in academic as in administrative and social matters, and there is something in the claim that heads keep the cards far too close to their chests, and do not always appear to realize the impact which decisions about curriculum and related matters may have on the community the school exists to serve. This was exemplified in secondary modern schools where heads did not believe in external examinations. They thought they had sound educational reasons on their side for supporting a freer curriculum, but these reasons were not apparent to parents and prospective employers who attached importance to more conventional records of attainment. The governors of such schools reflected this local concern, and brought pressure on the heads to introduce GCE courses. Their intervention was regarded by heads, so confronted, as unjustifiable invasions of their own sphere. Were they right? One chief education officer at least took the view that such interest on the part of governors was legitimate, and that it was for the head to justify his policy to them. He added that he would back up the head, but he was not prepared to tell the governors they were out of order. Another chief education officer went further and expressed the view that there was no general aspect of a school's activities in which governors could not claim a prima facie interest, and that his heads would be justified in complaining about their intervention only if they started to ask questions about individual pupils or teachers, or if they refused to accept the head's explanation of some purely professional matter which they had raised.

The discussion of examination results is a matter of contention. When they are included in the head's report, some governors are reluctant to ask for more information in case the head jumps down their throat; they are permitted only to express approval of outstanding achievement, while any form of criticism is regarded as quite unjustifiable. Thus they cannot compare current and previous performances, or discuss a relatively poor showing in this or that subject. Heads meet these criticisms by claiming that governors are inclined to look on examination results as material for a league table, and to make quite unwarranted comparisons between schools organized on quite different lines. They are also concerned to protect individual members of staff from attacks by outsiders, who might, in extreme cases, propose that the head of an allegedly unsatisfactory department should be called before the governors to be reported for poor examinations results. The weakness of teachers or departments was regarded as a matter of entirely professional concern; a head might decide to seek advice or support from the chief education officer or a subject adviser, but did not consider that he was accountable in any respect to a lay body on such matters.

There is obvious force in these arguments; at the same time, if some branches of the school's work appear to be consistently weaker or less successful than others, it might be argued that this is a matter of public concern on which a lay body has a claim to be heard. While accepting the head's final responsibility, governors may still be entitled to ask for his observations, or for an explanation. There are a number of instances of heads being prepared to discuss their school's academic shortcomings with their governors, pointing out that a poor examination performance has resulted, for example, from the authority's refusal to authorize an extra specialist appointment, from inability to attract candidates of good calibre to a school without inadequate equipment, or from the appointment, in which the governors may have shared, of a candidate who has failed to live up to early promise. These instances suggest that there are good reasons for acquainting governors with a school's academic achievements and deficiencies, if only to show that administrative decisions on such matters as staffing ratios or salary gradings may have tangible educational results. In any event governors get only a very one-sided picture of a school if they are not shown something of its difficulties as well as of its achievements.

Where heads are prepared to take governors into their confidence over academic matters, the latter generally respond by accepting the head's ultimate responsibility for deciding what is to be taught and how it is to be taught. This, however, need not debar governors from making suggestions of their own, and in two secondary modern schools studied they had pressed respectively for the introduction of a second language and for the retention of French (which the head was thinking of dropping). In both cases the heads regarded the governors' interest as entirely legitimate.

The influence which a governing body can exercise by its mere presence is seen from an interview with a head appointed to preside over the amalgamation of two schools with differing outlooks and traditions. He had had to introduce a number of fresh practices in his first year, and had gained his governors' support in every case. He intended to recast the curriculum to give greater scope to the less academic pupils, whom he considered to have suffered under the previous regime. However, he thought that this departure from tradition might antagonize some of his governors, coming on top of his other innovations, and he was prepared to leave the curriculum much as it was for the time being so that his governors did not have too many changes to digest at once.

Elsewhere, however, governors' intervention had been distinctly unhappy, particularly where individual governors had bees in their bonnets or an imperfect acquaintance with contemporary education, or where they used their formal responsibility for the curriculum as a justification for forcing their own views on the head. One head, for example, told his governors about a scheme, which had been in operation for some months, through which the boys were using the local bowling alley as part of their sports programme. One governor took exception to this on the grounds that bowling was a sport with the wrong associations, and forced the head to withdraw this activity from the curriculum. The head said that he is now very careful what he tells his governors, and this account is paralleled by several more where heads have regretted ever discussing curricular matters with their governors. Nor should we omit to mention the sheer ignorance or perversity with which some heads are confronted on the part of their governors; as, for example, that of the governor who queried the need for a Latin teacher in a grammar school, or that of another who objected to the introduction of shorthand and typing because there was a private teacher of these subjects in the town.

Some heads actively seek to stimulate the interest of their governors in curriculum matters. At some schools it is customary for heads of departments or other teachers to give a talk to the governors about their own work, and to answer questions. Occasionally heads go further than this, and arrange demonstration lessons for governors so that they can see for themselves how new and expensive equipment is being used, and with what results, or what precisely is involved in new teaching techniques or projects.

DISCIPLINARY ISSUES

According to the standard clauses in articles of government, heads are responsible for the discipline within the school, but are invariably required to consult or inform the governors on suspending a pupil. Consultation frequently takes the form of the head notifying the chairman, who may call an emergency meeting of the governors, or simply report the matter at the next meeting. The role of the governors on such occasions is normally confined to endorsing action already taken, as it is generally firmly held that the head should be supported and his authority reinforced where necessary. This tendency can be illustrated by reference to a case of suspension in which one body of governors was more actively involved.

The head in one school had forbidden the wearing of badges, except those of two organizations with which the school itself was connected. This ban was imposed because of the practice of collecting badges and then holding competitions to see how many could be sported at once on school blazers. At one period, however, the wearing of CND badges was widespread, but this in turn stimulated the production of 'Up with the Bomb' badges. One morning 20 sixth formers turned up wearing CND badges. The head decided that matters had gone too far and invoked his ban. The sixth formers removed their badges with the exception of three, two of whom conformed, with letters of apology, after they had been suspended for a short time. The third held out and was suspended officially. His parents appealed and his case was argued at a special meeting of the governors which heard both the boy and the head. The governors took the view that the school rules were a matter for the head and that, if he chose to insist that only certain badges should be worn on the school premises, he should be supported. Far from being persecutors of CND, the governing body included three active CND supporters. After this the boy removed his badge, only to be expelled a year later for refusing to conform to another school rule.

There appeared to be few cases, save for suspensions, where governors were involved collectively and officially in matters of school discipline. Most heads took the view that its enforcement rests fairly and squarely on their own shoulders and that, if the governors are invoked as a court of appeal, they will almost certainly regard it as their prime duty to support the head. However, it is possible that in certain circumstances governors might not be content with this role; if, for example, they thought that a head had acted too harshly or precipitately, or had handled a disciplinary problem in an unsatisfactory manner; or if they considered school rules or their execution to be altogether perverse or unreasonable. Even so, it is difficult to imagine their refusing to back up the head's action except in the most extreme cases; a more likely outcome would be for them to suggest that next time the head would be well advised to handle matters differently.

. Occasionally governors, and especially chairmen, intervene on a personal basis. For example, after the head had tried unsuccessfully to talk to the uncooperative father of a boy who had been giving a lot of trouble, the chairman went round for a straight man-to-man talk which succeeded in changing the father's attitude. This and other instances suggest that there is a case for having a person or group of persons associated with the school but not acting simply as its emissaries (or as those of the LEA), who will be able to intervene on behalf of the school with parents. Some governors thought that not enough was made of their potential value in this connexion. They complained, for example, that they were not told when children were brought before the courts. They thought that they might be able to exert some influence on such occasions, especially if they were well-known in the locality. They also thought that heads were too inclined to pretend that all was sweetness and light in their schools, when they should be more willing to admit and discuss the problems raised by individual pupils or groups of pupils.

SUPPORT FOR HEADS

It was claimed again and again by heads, in the course of interviews, that their work necessarily imposed on them a certain degree of isolation and that a sympathetic governing body and, above all, a sympathetic chairman of governors can be of very real help in times of difficulty. In particular, heads of schools in difficult areas felt the need for help and support from their governors, but more often than not did not get it. They desperately wanted support, even though they were not sure just what form this support might take. They wanted assistance in overcoming the apathy of parents and children, and often in combating strong delinquent tendencies in the neighbourhood; and, more positively, they wanted someone—anyone—outside the education service to know about what they were trying to do in their schools, and what changes they were making and why. Clearly there was a failure of communication between heads and governors of these schools, as many governors were convinced that they were quite active and maintained that they went along regularly to talk to the head. They did not see anything more they could do.

Contact between heads and their chairmen varies very much from one authority to another. It appears to be minimal when the chairman is, by prescription, custom, or accident, a member of the local education authority, but even in these circumstances some heads find it useful to keep in touch with their chairmen about day-to-day matters and thus reduce the isolation they sometimes feel. The most favourable situation occurs when a governing body contains people with a variety of outlook and experience, and at least one or two members who can put up some sort of intellectual challenge to the head. It is also important that the head should make a conscious effort to build up good relationships with his governors, irrespective of his estimate of their intellectual capacity. An able head can become very frustrated by the petty restrictions imposed by some authorities, but this frustration can be largely mitigated if he had built up a good relationship with his governors, so that they help him to use his own judgment. Regional differences matter. One head expressed the difference between northern downrightness and southern smoothness in the following terms: 'My last set of governors in the north seemed much more politically conscious than my present governors appear to be, and I often felt that politics played far too large a part . . . Meetings were held in the Council Chamber every month in the evening and were vigorous, down-to-earth, uncompromising occasions. Everything about my present authority seems much more relaxed and genteel, and I could not easily say what are the political views (if any) of most of my governors. Meetings are held once a term, in the afternoon, at the school, and I think they will be pleasant occasions. But I think I shall miss the straight talking and the battles of my previous authority, and I shall have to be on my guard lest I become soft. I hope there will always be a gadfly among us who will keep us on our toes, keep us arguing and restless.'

GOVERNING BODIES AND THEIR LOCAL EDUCATION AUTHORITIES

THE INFLUENCE OF GOVERNING BODIES

It is easy for chief education officers to claim that the views of governing bodies carry great weight with their authority, and are always given careful consideration even when they cannot be accepted. This is not borne out by the results of the HMM and NSH questionnaires.

Replies to both questionnaires show that there is remarkably little difference in the proportion of governing bodies considered effective in counties and county boroughs. It is not obvious, however, why respondents to the NSH questionnaire (mainly heads of non-selective schools) should have ascribed a higher degree of effectiveness to their governors than respondents to the HMM questionnaire (mainly heads of selective schools). The most probable explanation is that heads of secondary grammar schools and other selective schools have been generally able to get their voices heard unaided, whereas heads of other schools feel that their governors can do more for them.

In the course of the area studies, several instances were recorded, where the intervention of the governors clearly seems to have produced results where the head on his own has not been

Heads views on the effectiveness of their governing bodies in respect of influence on local education authorities

Views expressed HMM questionnaire	Heads in Counties	Heads in County Boroughs
Governors effective	18	19
Governors ineffective	60	46
Individual governors effective	11	11
LEA members on governing body effective	43	—
	132	76
NSH questionnaire		
Governors effective	80	42
Governors ineffective	82	38
Chairman effective	8	5
LEA members on governing body effective	42	23
	212	108

(In the NSH questionnaire, attention was directed at the chairman as a potentially influential member, rather than at any individual member of the governing body.)

successful. The effectiveness of the governors' intervention was confirmed by the chief education officers of the authorities concerned.

A. According to the headmaster, the governors played an important part in checking the county surveyor's department which had decided, without consultation, to put a second road into the school grounds. This was strongly opposed by the head when he found out what was going on, and he took up the matter with his governors. They agreed with him and sent a deputation to County Hall, which resulted in a modification of the county's plans.

B. Two specific examples were quoted by the headmaster of this school. On one occasion an item in the minor building programme had been held up through what he thought was administrative incompetence at County Hall. The head himself contacted the office to try to get something done, but got nowhere until the chairman of governors (a county councillor) spoke to the chief education officer and the chief architect. This got things moving.

The second occasion concerned the lights in the hall, which had been approved in the estimates but were not installed for some time, although it was known that they were needed urgently. The head could not get anything done until the chairman wrote and complained.

C. The head and the governors were very angry when a proposed gymnasium was dropped from the plan to extend the school building. After pressure from the governors a meeting was called to discuss the plans with senior officers of the authority. The result was a decision to proceed with the extension to the existing accommodation, but not to include the gymnasium. Although it was thought that this decision to get on with the extension would have been reached without the governors' intervention, their chairman thought it important that a public protest had been made through them. If the complaining had been left to the head, the chairman did not think that the authority would have sent such important people down to explain and defend their policy. The head, as an employee of the authority, could not protest so strongly as the governors who were independent of it.

D. The authority had planned two single-sex comprehensive schools which could collaborate in work at fifth and sixth form levels and in social activities. The buildings were separate but on the same campus. The boys' school was completed first, but due to pressure of places was opened as a mixed school. Three years later, while the girls' school was still being built, political control of the education committee changed hands and it was decided to turn both schools, when finally opened, into a single mixed comprehensive school, against the advice of the chief education officer. Objections to the amalgamation were made by 40 local electors, but some of the governors took the lead in organizing a counter-petition in favour of the new decision which was signed by nearly 2,000 local residents. This petition was sent to the Department of Education and Science, who thought this demonstration of public feeling so overwhelming that it provided their main reason for approving the authority's decision. (The matter had to be referred to the Department because it involved the technical closure of an existing school.)

E. The education committee had decided in favour of converting a mixed school into a single-sex school. The head was against the proposal, and with the backing of his governors he got the decision reversed.

F. The heads of two old schools in poor areas both felt that they had received better treatment through governors, who were also members of the education committee, looking after their interests. Both schools had been granted very favourable staffing ratios. One head on taking up his appointment had demanded £1,000 on the spot to improve the school's equipment. This was granted though the school was officially scheduled for closure (and had been for years) and the authority had been reluctant to spend money on what it regarded as a dying school.

G. When a school moved to the premises of another school the governors were said to have played a decisive part in getting an equipment allowance for it. This was an unusual achievement since such an allowance is normally granted only to a school moving into new premises, and not when it takes over the premises of another school.

Such examples are relatively uncommon, as they are concerned with major decisions which have to be taken only infrequently in the life of a school. However, they do suggest both the potential and the actual effectiveness of intervention by governors. It is significant that the examples quoted are drawn from a variety of authorities and by no means only from large scattered counties. Indeed, three examples come from small or medium-sized county boroughs—precisely the type of authority where chief education officers are inclined to argue that governors are superfluous because the needs of the school are well known to the authority.

SECONDARY REORGANIZATION

Consultation with governors was expressly advised in Circular 10/65 and, indeed, it is difficult to conceive how, if they have any influence at all, they can fail to be involved in schemes of reorganization which may affect the very existence of their schools as individual units.

The evidence available from the research study on this important issue is neither as complete nor as systematically based as might be hoped. Chief education officers who were interviewed were asked how far governing bodies had been consulted in respect of plans for reoganization. At the time, however, many authorities had not progressed far in preparing their schemes and all their chief education officers could say was that governing bodies would be consulted at the appropriate time. In only two counties did chief education officers take pains to stress that ultimate decisions rested firmly with the authority, and that governors were more likely to be informed about the county's plans than to be consulted. In the rest it was assumed that governors had a right to be brought into any process of consultation set up. At this point it is necessary to underline the crucial importance of the role of the chief education officer in preparing a preliminary plan, even when he is apparently given very firm directions by his committee as to the desired method of reorganization. The chief education officer and his staff are the key group in so far as they have exclusive access to the relevant data, and alone are in a position to work out the practicability of different schemes and their educational implications for individual schools, to negotiate with DES on the acceptability of various proposals, and to present the elected members with a clear choice. Frequently, this preliminary work done in the office limits severely the choices in theory open to the local educational authority or governing bodies, and the solution put forward by the officers may, in fact, be the only practicable one. This does not mean that discussions and consultations with teachers associations and representatives with governors and with committee members are a waste of time. 'Practicability' has to be proved in political as well as in administrative terms; and political 'practicability' can only be tested if the professional administrators have fully assessed and reported on alternative proposals.

In one or two LEAs governing bodies were brought in at a very early stage—rather too early, in fact, for one chief education officer, who had not yet formulated his own views in detail. In this authority governing bodies were provided with details of the options suggested in circular 10/65, with a summary of the general advantages and disadvantages of each. They were then given a completely free hand, together with managing bodies, parents' associations, old scholars and teaching staff. Practically every organization consulted made its views felt, and it was then left to the authority to sort out a mass of frequently irreconcilable recommendations and to prepare a plan which would commend itself to as many parties as possible. Most parties would have been more or less satisfied with a system of junior comprehensive schools for the years 11–16 and a sixth form college: but the chief education officer had now decided, largely as a result of the discussions held with governing bodies, that a three-tier system had much more to commend it. The education committee accepted proposals for the two-tier system but the county council, much to the relief of the chief education officer, reversed this decision in favour of the three-tier system. The chief education officer thought on reflection that he should not have given governing bodies such an entirely free hand originally, and that he would have done better to stress the advantages of the three-tier system without, of course, hindering governors if they wished to recommend some alternative. Other chief education officers said that governing bodies thought that a completely open discussion lacked reality, and that their views would have more point if directed to specific proposals, the implications of which had already been fully worked out.

In many counties there was room for flexibility, and chief education officers said that it had been possible to accommodate specific proposals, e.g. for a sixth form college, if local opinion was solidly and enthusiastically in favour, even though they did not consider it the best solution for the county generally. Some governing bodies were flattered to think that they were setting the pace by starting an educational experiment. Chief education officers felt that when governors had been consulted, their views had generally affected the final outcome even if only in minor particulars. On the other hand, there is no doubt that many chief education officers would take it as a reflection on their own professional competence if proposals which they had fully worked out could not be defended successfully in front of apprehensive or hostile governors. The most intractable category, according to chief education officers, were the governing bodies of some grammar schools who thought they had most to lose from reorganization. There was often much nailing of colours to the mast and talk of dying in the last ditch, especially in the early stages, and governing bodies of voluntary aided or controlled schools could stimulate resistance on the part of their county colleagues. Sometimes they could find themselves in illogical positions: refusing at any price to be expanded into an orthodox comprehensive as this was too much of a leap in the dark, but being ready to form the top tier (13–18) of a three-tier system which, as one chief education officer rightly argued, was much more of a leap in the dark. Some chief education officers claimed to make grammar school governors more receptive by consulting them not on their own but together with governors of neighbouring non-selective schools. In this way they could be made aware of the educational needs of the area as a whole, and of the more useful part which their school could play if it were reorganized.

Some more detailed information of the extent to which governing bodies were consulted was gained through the area studies. Only in one of the counties visited were governors not involved. In this county, totally covered by divisional executives and excepted districts, working parties of teacher representatives and members of the divisional executives and excepted districts were already preparing their reorganization plans before the circular was issued. Just how far governors were consulted depended very much on the particular division. In those visited this amounted to very little. The official view was that it would have been impossible for each governing body to have worked out a plan for its own school since it could not take a broad view of the needs of the whole division. The county had instructed divisional officers to consult with the governors, but just what this meant was not clear. The majority of heads and governors interviewed felt that they had not been consulted, and consultation with parents was also minimal. The general inference was that neither parents nor governors were in a position to understand the problems of secondary reorganization, and the simplest solution by far was not to involve them in it.

In one area governors had been consulted in so far as they had had opportunities to make comments on the draft plans. However, it was generally felt that there had been a 'semblance of consultation' rather than consultation proper. A good example of how far from reality consultation could be was given in one area where the plans discussed at a joint meeting held for governors, heads and other interested parties were not the plans which eventually appeared in the draft proposals: this was justified on the grounds that, after the joint meeting, further information came to light which made the original draft proposals unsuitable, and there had been no time for further consultation. Although the chief education officer and his staff and the members of the education committee believed that they had acted democratically, this was not the generally accepted view.

In three other counties governing bodies had been consulted either individually about their own schools, or together where proposals affected a group of schools. Where governors were consulted there seems to have been more readiness to accept the authority's plans even where these differed from the governors' own views. Sometimes governors do seem to have been able to influence the authority's proposals. In one area (after their first suggestions had been rejected by the education committee) the governing bodies of the schools affected by the plan got together and sent in unanimously agreed proposals. The influence at county level of the chairman of governors of one of the schools was seen as instrumental in getting the decision of the education committee reversed in the full county council meeting, while the united backing of the governors was thought to be an important factor.

This authority had previously burnt its fingers with a suddenly produced proposal for the closure of a very small grammar school and was particularly anxious to ensure full local consultation in the future.

In county boroughs, the extent and nature of consultation with governors depends on the structure of school government. Thus, in authorities where the governing body is virtually a sub-committee of the education committee, overlap of membership is such that consultation is precluded. In authorities with governing bodies for individual schools or small groups of schools consultation can have some meaning. But in the authorities visited in the course of the area studies the view taken was that governors had little part to play in planning the reorganization of secondary education. In one authority with governing bodies for individual schools, the heads thought that reorganization was a matter they should discuss with their governors, although they could not go so far as to seek to enlist their active support against the authority's stated policy. But three heads said they would be prepared to ask their boards to pass resolutions condemning a plan—and this even though among their governors were committee members who had been involved in working party discussions, or who were expected to be bound by committee decisions.

In comparison with the part played by other agencies, such as teachers' consultative committees, local press campaigns and agitation by parent groups the role played by governors in respect of secondary reorganization is insignificant. This is not to say that there are not a substantial number of occasions on which individual governors, or groups of governors, have not played a key role in local disputes. But whereas in many authorities teachers have played a full part in consultation, often serving on working parties set up to study schemes of reorganization, governors, as such, are rarely called upon in the same way. This is not surprising, since in so many authorities, the core of all governing bodies is formed of councillors and committee members who are already heavily involved in preparing the overall plan for their authority.

COMMUNICATION BETWEEN LOCAL
EDUCATION AUTHORITIES AND GOVERNORS

If governors are to perform their functions adequately a first essential is that they should know what those are, and be guided in their performance. By and large little is done in either direction, but there are a number of authorities, mainly counties, which have given their attention to this matter. Some of these issue handbooks which present a broad outline of the tasks of the local education authority itself, describe the formal constitution and activities of governors and governing bodies, deal with the special place accorded to the head in relation to governors and, in some cases, give an overview of the school system as a whole. Such guidance can be invaluable both to governors, heads and officials, especially where the more informal and personal aspects of governors' activities are concerned. One or two divisional officers have, in addition, prepared their own notes of guidance to supplement those issued by the county authority. These can also be of great value, since they can refer to local issues in a manner impossible in publications intended for a wider circulation.

There is, however, another need: this is the need to keep governors fully informed during their tenure of office. This is met even less adequately than the needs of newly appointed governors. One or two authorities issue news letters or bulletins, which cover topics ranging from educational experiments to an analysis of the authority's estimates or the role of local inspectors. Some authorities make available to governors circulars primarily intended for the guidance of heads and other teachers. These may convey no more than information relating to administrative procedures, as for example, the ordering of supplies on a prescribed form by a certain date. For governors, of course, such information is of little assistance unless linked with general information on school finance and supplies.

One or two authorities have regular area conferences for their governors. This may extend over half a day or a whole day, with the first part devoted to talks by members of the education committee, by the chief education officer and by members of his staff. These are generally followed by general discussion. In addition to these 'official' conferences, political parties in some areas hold meetings for groups of governors which serve a similar purpose, although they have a decidedly political flavour and more time may be spent arguing about major policy issues than discussing the matters of detail on which information can be so difficult to get.

In the main, the most important and potentially effective channel of communication between the local education authority and governors—and this is true in all types of authority—is the officer who acts as clerk. In all authorities except a few counties he is generally a high- or medium-ranking officer of the authority; only a minority of counties continue the older practice of local clerking, on the grounds that this enhances the status of governing bodies. This does not, however, ensure that the governors are provided by authoritative advice and information at the moments when they may most need them. Another kind of weakness appears in clerking when too junior an officer is entrusted with this duty. He can neither enjoy the confidence of the head, nor be expected to interpret the authority to the governors or the governors to the authority. But no matter how able, or how experienced an officer acting as clerk may be, his contribution must depend on extent to which a defined place is accorded to school governors within the overall pattern of administration in the authority.

6 The Management of Primary Schools

Both historical and administrative factors account for the substantial differences in the approach to the management of primary schools and the government of secondary schools. Historically, as has already been shown, they have very different roots and this is reflected in the status of the Rules of Management of Primary Schools and the Articles of Government of Secondary Schools. Administratively, the former are the sole responsibility of the local education authority, whilst the latter require the approval of the Department of Education and Science.

STRUCTURE AND COMPOSITION

It has been rare for local education authorities to develop systems of primary school management that take into account the individuality of their schools. There are far more primary schools, their needs appear more uniform and their internal structure is simpler than that of secondary schools. To provide them all with their own managing bodies would, it is claimed, make far too heavy demands on administrative and clerical staff and present insuperable problems in finding suitable people prepared to serve on them. Except in the more rural county areas, therefore, the general rule is for primary schools in a given area to be grouped together; in some cases, this means all primary schools in the authority.

On the other hand, local interest in primary schools is often very strong. In rural areas the head is frequently at a focal point in the community, and in the case of church schools, the managers themselves may be well known because of their connection with their church. In urban areas, the primary school years are often those during which parents feel themselves most closely linked with their children's schooling. As a result there has been, at least in recent years, a growing demand for parental participation in primary school management, fostered by organized groups, such as the local Associations for the Advancement of State Education and Federation of Parent-Teacher Associations.

Our studies of the government of secondary schools covered every authority in the country and were supported by detailed case studies. Primary school management, however, was a subsidiary, though an important, element in the research project, and our first-hand investigations were more limited in scope. Nevertheless, they took the form of interviews with the chief education officers of 27 counties, 25 county boroughs and 18 outer London boroughs. These form a substantial proportion of all local education authorities and, since they include authorities of all sizes and counties with varying patterns of subordinate administration, the material collected can be taken as broadly representative. In addition we had made available to us the results of a survey of the management and government of schools made by the Schools Council of the Church of England Board of Education. A third source was interviews with the regional officers of a major teachers' association.

In the county boroughs and the outer London boroughs managing bodies for individual schools or for small groups of schools are rare. Among the county boroughs visited, sixteen appoint a sub-committee of the education committee to act as the managing body of *all* their schools, three had a system of grouping several primary schools with one or more secondary schools, five had managing bodies dealing with groups of schools, and only one had set up a managing body for each of its primary schools. The Outer London boroughs were similarly divided between those who favour grouping or the sub-committee system.

The situation is quite different in the counties, where there is virtual unanimity among chief education officers as to the desirability of each school having its own body of managers. In the more rural areas conditions favour this and grouping is rare: in towns, however, individual managing bodies are frequent, although some chief education officers have had to agree to grouping in some of the larger or expanding minor authorities. Most counties are prepared to give some weight to the views of local councils on arrangements for primary school management, especially where these are former Part III authorities. Excepted Districts often go their own way, even if this involves doing what the county regards as undesirable.

In many respects the formal status of managing bodies for primary schools, as measured by provisions of the rules of management, was generally similar to that of the authority's governing bodies for secondary schools; some six out of eight authorities provided for the submission of estimates by individual bodies of managers, seven had identical arrangements for the appointment of heads of primary and secondary schools, and seven again provided that in both primary and secondary schools the managers should have the general oversight of the school and its curriculum. In practice, however, these provisions are frequently dead letters. There seems to be general agreement that it is out of the question to prepare estimates for each primary school, while with regard to the general oversight of the school and its curriculum the managers are solely dependent on the head and what he chooses to put in his report.

In the counties studied the status of managers, measured in terms of their formal powers, was less than that of governors. Thus only rarely were they accorded any part in the preparation of estimates or in the 'general oversight of the curriculum'. In most instances, too, their part in the appointment of head teachers was less considerable than that played by governors.

In any case, so little attention is paid to rules of management that some still retain curious relics from the past. Rules are found providing for managers to inspect stock books and registers, and to ensure that the school-keeper exercises due economy in the use of fuel and cleaning materials (if exercised, this latter function would surely make the managers most unpopular in the worst of the winter!). The reservations expressed elsewhere on the short-comings of articles of government as a guide to what actually happens apply in even greater measure to rules of management.

CHIEF EDUCATION OFFICERS' VIEWS

The utility of managing bodies is not rated highly by the chief education officers of urban authorities, particularly in those where there is some system of visiting schools by individual education committee members. This is generally considered to have many advantages, in that it enables councillors to get to know the schools and to deal with local enquiries and complaints. Evidence of interest on the part of the education committee improves the morale of the school, and it is helpful if a head can unburden himself to a sympathetic and influential listener. Moreover, some chief education officers claim that they make a point of visiting all their primary schools from time to time, or at least ensuring that their senior colleagues do so. In these circumstances it is argued that the paramount need is not so much to strengthen the link between the school and the local community, as to ensure that the schools have direct access to individual members of the education committee, and to the chief education officer and his staff. Furthermore, if it is admitted that there is a need for some person or persons to perform an ambassadorial function on behalf of the school this can be discharged very well by councillors.

Still greater reservations are expressed by chief education officers in boroughs where schools are grouped for management purposes, although it is argued that such an arrangement is better than the single sub-committee system, in that managers have some kind of link with individual schools and their heads. There was a strong body of opinion that managing bodies, whatever their form, had little place in compact communities, where councillors, committee members and officers were in close touch with the schools.

On the other hand, in the counties chief education officers were emphatic that the need to have a machinery for wide lay participation in education is valid in a large measure in urban areas as well. There was, they held, no overwhelming reason for assuming that conditions in counties and county boroughs were so entirely different that no common assumptions held good, although they were not unaware of the grounds upon which some of their colleagues in the county boroughs rejected this view. A basic difference was that the county boroughs, where they saw any justification at all for school managers, considered that this lay in providing a direct link between the education committee and the schools, while the counties felt that the need was to provide a general link between the school and the local community.

The greatest stumbling block to the institution of highly developed systems of school management in the urban authorities is the administrative burden which they are held to impose, and which are considered to be out of all proportion to the benefits which might result. This argument is not seriously advanced against the establishment of governing bodies for secondary schools, but it clearly has some force when the number of schools involved may be four or five times as large and when the expenditure of the time of highly qualified staff and other resources must be quite considerable.

In some authorities meetings of the primary schools sub-committee are sometimes cancelled for lack of business, and elsewhere they last for only a few minutes. Some authorities have tried in turn both a sub-committee system and a system of grouping, but have not considered that the results justified the latter. Great stress is laid on the arguments that the needs of primary schools are simpler, and that their heads are less demanding than their secondary colleagues.

The one county borough visited, which had a system of individual managing bodies, has solved some of the administrative problems by designating one of the managers as clerk, with responsibility for the preparation of agendas, minutes and communications to and from the authority. In the larger authorities at least, there would appear to be scope for the flexible deployment of administrative and professional staff, so as to allow for the establishment of a section devoted to school management and, presumably, for school government also.

CLERKING ARRANGEMENTS

In the counties there is great divergence of views on the best arrangements for clerking managing bodies. Similar counties may opt for entirely opposite arrangements. Some scattered rural counties, for example, have all primary schools clerked from the education office, whilst others which are much more compact attach importance to having one of the managers acting as clerk. Still others have hybrid systems, particularly if there are a number of divisional executives within their areas. Sometimes a county will take over local clerkships as these fall vacant through death, removal or resignation. The arguments for central clerking are that it keeps managers in touch with the office, and enables authoritative answers to be given to their queries at meetings. It ensures that managing bodies actually meet, and is good training for the administrative assistants who are sometimes used for this work. Local clerks may be unbusinesslike or, at the other extreme, legalistic, and the extra administrative cost may be justified by the wider needs of the county's administration as a whole. In favour of local clerks, it is argued that the administrative burden of official clerking would be enormous and not justified in terms of the amount of business transacted. Some chief education officers also think that managers' discussions would be inhibited if their representative was present at the meeting, particularly if he perceived his function as being to telling managers what they could not have or do. However, as in secondary schools, it is certainly possible for the clerk to regard himself as serving his managing or governing body at their meeting, rather than as an emissary from the Education Department. The problems produced by these conflicting claims on the clerk's loyalties seem to be much exaggerated. They are not apparent on secondary school governing bodies.

Some counties try to meet the acknowledged disadvantages of

local clerking by giving newly appointed clerks guidance on the preparation of agendas and minutes, and on means of keeping in touch with the local education authority. Sometimes a modest honorarium is paid to local clerks, and in this way they are reminded of their responsibilities to the county. However, even those authorities which are in favour of local clerking agree that it is not easy to keep track of every managing body in the county, and that there may well be managing bodies which do not hold their statutory three meetings each year. Indeed some managing bodies have been reported (sometimes by vigilant or desperate groups of parents) as not having met for over two years. The limitations of having a completely amateur clerk can be avoided if, as in one county, members of the Education Department staff act as clerks in their spare time. It is notable that chief education officers with experience of both systems tend to prefer professional clerking in spite of increased administrative costs. Indeed, it may well be the case that professional clerking does not cost much more in effect, especially if a local clerk is an unbusinesslike person with whom correspondence over the simplest item becomes protracted. Careful planning may enable a clerk to attend two or three managing bodies in a day, even in the more scattered counties, and deal with other matters at the schools at the same time.

RECRUITMENT OF MANAGERS

Difficulty in recruiting people prepared to serve as managers is often put forward as a major obstacle by those authorities who have not developed adequate systems of school management. This difficulty does not exist, however, in a number of county areas, where would-be managers are sometimes reported as falling over themselves to serve. Nominations generally come through local councillors or aldermen, or from minor authorities in the area served. Sometimes they are scrutinized by the education committee, which may have to take a formal vote on disputed appointments. One county is able to go as far as to ask for details of prospective managers' interest in education, and to refer these back, if candidates do not seem to be suitably qualified. In some counties nominations are put forward by the chief education officer himself, as he comes across suitable people in his travels round the county. There is also some evidence to suggest that heads may have a considerable informal say in the selection of managers.

Great interest is always shown in the subject of parental membership of managing bodies. A few counties have some specific provision to this effect, but one goes to the other extreme and expressly forbids parents to serve on the managing body of their child's school. In this authority the view was taken that parents should voice their complaints and queries either to the head direct, or to their elected representative. Elsewhere it was reported that parents are commonly found on managing bodies and that it was almost impossible to avoid this in the villages. The balance of opinion was clearly in favour of having parents serving as managers, though some give this practice a more qualified welcome and a few have serious reservations, generally on the grounds that parents' interest is biased and transient and too dependent on what their child tells them, or on what the parents may mistakenly perceive to be in the true interests of the child.

It was claimed that managers could be helpful in introducing a new head to a village and could bring about a remarkably effective relationship between the parents and the school. Conversely a head could be in for a very unhappy time if some of the managers had actively opposed his appointment, or were not prepared to acquiesce in it. Where a head was appointed to a difficult school or one in a difficult area, managers could be a great source of encouragement; they could often see things from the point of view of the sensible parent, which was of great benefit. Heads who lived in the village school house and were a focal point for the local community were sometimes at the mercy of angry parents, and were glad to have managers on their side; while if, as increasingly occurs, the head did not live in the village, there might be still greater need for the managers to act as his eyes and ears. Service as managers had completely altered many peoples' attitudes to education and local administration and, as in secondary schools, they could be successful advocates of the need of their school within the county system of broad priorities. They could act as a first court of reference over disciplinary or other problems and parents were happy in knowing that local residents were involved with the school, and that managers could bring the authority's attention to matters affecting their own children. If managers were occasionally awkward, this is not an argument against them; the local education authority could be complacent as often as the local managers were bloody-minded.

In contrast the chief education officers in urban authorities perceive the needs of their schools, as we have seen, in altogether different terms. Most have a noticeable lack of enthusiasm for managing bodies and even where a system of grouping exists few positive advantages are claimed for it. The same basic attitude is apparent in the steps taken by the Outer London Boroughs after their inception. At the time of visiting, some eighteen months after they had been set up, the Boroughs had paid little attention to the pattern of school management. This, in itself, indicates their general lack of interest in this aspect of educational administration.

CHURCH OF ENGLAND SCHOOLS

So far attention has been paid only to the management of county primary schools. It was not, indeed, a main purpose of the research project to look into the management and government of voluntary schools. But the opportunity did present itself of studying some aspects of Church of England schools. This arose from discussions with members of a study group that had been set up by the Church of England Board of Education Schools Council to study the management and government of the Church's schools.

The enquiry that resulted took the form of a letter of enquiry addressed by the Secretary of the Council to all Diocesan Directors of Education. It was relatively limited in scope and sought to discover to what extent it was felt that each school should have its own individual body of managers and governors, the relationship existing between managing and governing bodies and both the Diocesan Education Committee and the local education authority, differences between rural and urban areas, the constitution of managing and governing bodies, and the kind of service to school and community that they performed.

In the event, because of the vast preponderance of primary over secondary schools, the replies received were in all cases couched in terms of the former rather than of the latter.

There was quite unanimous feeling in favour of each school, whether primary or secondary, having its own managing or governing body. The possible alternative, that of church schools in a locality forming a minor school system under the guidance of a Superintendent was not regarded with any degree of favour. It was indeed argued that 'such a suggestion would be abhorrent to the vast number of Head Teachers and Managers', and that grouping would 'lead to a loss of parish or local interest'. Another argument, of a more practical nature, is that rarely are enough church schools sufficiently close together for grouping to be practicable or useful. Moreover, grouping schools across parish boundaries presents obvious problems.

From the point of view of the Diocesan Directors, who occupy a particular sensitive position in this respect, relations between managers, local education authorities and Diocesan Education Boards are satisfactory. On the whole it is felt that diocesan centralization has not worked to the disadvantage of managing bodies: it can indeed act as a spur and the support that the diocesan authorities can give in financial matters, as regards building and in relation to appointments, is of very great help. One Diocesan Director wrote: 'I do not myself think that there is any real weakening of the independence and initiative of the managers because of the increase of diocesan interest in them. Indeed they invariably pester the Director to get them in a building programme long before he is ready for this or there is much prospect of anything happening. . . . What has clearly reduced their independence compared with their predecessors of earlier in this century and in the last, is government control of building projects, making them dependent on central approval and the fact that they cannot make improvements to their schools, even when they can find their share of the money, until they are permitted to do so by the Department certainly damps their enthusiasm.'

But this is not the unanimous view. One Diocesan Director wrote: 'Centralization on the Diocese especially in finance certainly has taken away a great deal of independence and initiative from Managers in this Diocese (as far as the Church's share is concerned). This means that Managers are comparatively sleeping partners. I have some examples where there is a personal relationship between a head and the Director as it were independently of the Managers. There are some cases, notably in Controlled Schools where a personal relationship between the head and the "Office" diminishes the effectiveness of the Managers. In some cases, especially where there is a dominant chairman, Managers take steps to limit this. In a town there will be a closer link between the head and the Office, and the Managers will tend to play a smaller part. In the country, the Managers will play a more important part.'

Little or no difficulty appears to be experienced in recruiting managers. In rural areas there appears to be sometimes a narrow area of recruitment from 'county' folk, farm owners and church-wardens. But this is by no means general. If any generalization is possible it is that managers represent a typical cross-section of Church membership. A usual practice in aided schools is for the four Foundation Managers to consist of the Incumbent, two representatives of the Parish Church Council and one representative of the Diocesan Education Committee. Often the Parochial Church Council nominates churchwardens. Local authorities vary in their approach to the appointment of representative managers. Most but not all tend to appoint councillors with sympathy for church schools frequently, and especially in controlled schools, representative managers take little interest.

One comment of interest is that the management of church schools is, apart from the incumbent, 'firmly in the hands of people who are not too heavily committed. Some of them are young and on the way up, others are those who have not been obviously successful in their profession, others are housewives and there are, as one would expect, the usual quota of unmarried ladies although I suspect that this kind of Manager is disappearing.'

There would appear to be a growing tendency for parents to serve as managers, although it may be that recent discussions have tended to make Diocesan Directors more aware of the parents who are serving on managing bodies. Opinion as to the desirability of parents serving is divided. Teacher representation, except for heads, was almost unanimously opposed. In the case of voluntary schools, there is an obvious difficulty in designating further categories of managers. There is the knotty problem of deciding whether a teacher member should be designated by the church or the local education authority. A similar difficulty could arise in the case of parental representation. In voluntary schools any revision of the structure of managing or governing bodies brings in the whole question of control within the voluntary sector.

There can be no doubt that managers of church primary schools, especially in rural areas, are felt to be an integral part of the pattern of educational administration. Their legal powers assure them of such a place. But, in addition, reference to replies to the enquiry show that their involvement in appointments, in the oversight of their schools and in dealings with both church and local education authorities is considerable. There is, however, sharply conflicting assessments of their community role. In some areas it is claimed that they are known by the neighbourhood and do, in a sense, represent the school to it. In others, and, as one might expect, mostly in urban areas, they are as anonymous as most of the elected representatives.

A SAFEGUARD FOR TEACHERS

Whilst it is argued that managers are keen and interested in both school and church, the most frequent lament is of their lack of knowledge and understanding of educational and administrative issues. The regional officers of the teachers' association consulted stated that where the local incumbent was chairman of the managers he might not be sufficiently aware of the differences in the status of a county school and that of an aided school. They felt that there was still a certain amount of clerical harassment of village teachers and that this, at least in some areas, had not diminished over the years. It was difficult to say just how often this occurred, as the officers pointed out that they might be aware of only the most flagrant cases, and that less extreme instances of improper influence might never come to their notice.

Tensions certainly were sometimes apparent, particularly in growing villages with articulate or militant parents who did not favour denominational religious education, and who sent their children to the local voluntary aided school on sufferance. Such parents reported obstacles being put in the way of withdrawal from worship or religious education; hostility on the part of foundation managers or Diocesan authorities to approaches which the parents regarded as showing entirely legitimate interest or concern ('this is a Church school and parental representation on the managing body is none of your business'); and reluctance by the local education authority to intervene in reply to parental or local requests, particularly when the managers' authority was being challenged. The situation may arise where one or two foundation managers run the school in their own way. This is most likely to happen when a foundation manager acts as correspondent, and when minutes are not circulated but merely kept in a book at the home of the correspondent. Under such circumstances, where there is no direct link between the managers and the local education authority, there is no guarantee that managers' meetings are being held regularly, that necessary business is transacted properly, or that managers are appointed in accordance with agreed procedure. Occasional cases have been reported of representative managers being kept very much in the dark, and not even being allowed to see minutes of previous meetings. In one no doubt extreme instance, the same person was reported as serving both as a foundation manager nominated by the Parochial Church Council, and as a representative manager nominated by the Parish Council for a period of seven years. This was discovered and action taken only when a group of dissatisfied parents managed to obtain, after several months delay and with the help of a solicitor, a copy of the Instrument of Management.

The regional officers of the teachers association pointed out that their intervention on behalf of teachers only touch a tiny minority of voluntary and county schools. There were, for instance, only isolated instances of managers asking improper questions when interviewing candidates for appointments. One particularly far-fetched instance was quoted of 'a Lady Bountiful in a southern county who asked a prospective head for his views on foxhunting, and whether he would be prepared to clear the gutters of the school house and look after the swimming pool in the absence of a caretaker.' Their very rarity makes such instances memorable. Less extreme questions of doubtful validity were asked more often: for example, whether candidates' wives went out to work and whether candidates could play the organ, or were prepared to run a scout troop. In spite of their shortcomings, which could occasionally be appalling, the squirearchy were generally regarded as surprisingly enlightened in many ways. The officers reserved their strongest criticisms for a few managing or governing bodies composed of shop stewards, who thought they could bring the militant attitudes of the shop floor into issues affecting their school.

INFORMATION AND GUIDANCE

There is one common element in views expressed by chief education officers, Diocesan directors of education and the regional officers of the teachers' association. This is the insistence on the need for both information and guidance to be made freely available to managers. Nevertheless, efforts in this direction are sporadic, although five of the 27 counties visited issue handbooks, which are greatly appreciated. Two local education authorities hold conferences for groups of managers and the chief education officers were so enthusiastic about these that it is worth describing them in detail:

In Authority A, the Chief Education Officer felt strongly the danger of individual managers not having contact with the authority and its officers. There was a need for means by which chairmen of committees and he himself might meet managers informally to discuss plans and grievances, and to improve their interest in and information on local schools. The right kind of background would be provided by an exhibition of schools' work, where those concerned could meet for an afternoon and compare notes over tea. The system of conferences that resulted, and which had been held for ten years, seemed to have paid off. With six or seven groups of primary schools meeting at a time it took three years to cover the county.

In Authority B, meetings of all managers were held after the triennial elections. This gave new managers a considerable amount of informal guidance, and old managers a chance of keeping up to date. The chief education officer said that the event was welcomed by managers and that this was borne out by the attendance figures. Meetings were held at a school which would be especially interesting to managers, for example, a school for handicapped children, or a new comprehensive school. In the morning the managers would listen to two or three speakers, break for lunch, and in the afternoon there would be a question and answer session. The speakers would talk on matters of general educational interest. The chief education officer in his talk might incorporate some hints on minor administrative detail (for example, the inadvisability of sending an omnibus letter dealing with several distinct issues to County Hall, as this would cause difficulties and was likely to lead to delay). It was hoped that the morning talks would spark off questions for the afternoon session, answered by a panel which included the chief education officer, the chairman of the education committee and two heads.

Another County issues a special bulletin to managers and governors on general educational matters twice a year, while a few others let the clerks to managing bodies see the monthly schools bulletins sent to heads and which are concerned mainly with current administrative detail.

There are somewhat similar instances of provision being made by Diocesan Education Committees. In one diocese training evenings have been arranged for Incumbents and for the complete Managing Bodies. These take place in different parts of the diocese and information is given on the routine matters of what it means to be a Manager, the role of the Diocesan Education Committee in relation to the local education authorities, together with some explanation of the place and function of the dual system in the educational life of the country. In another diocese a schools newsletter goes out every term to managers and staffs of aided and controlled schools. This, beside general information, gave guidance as regards administrative procedures, the progress of school building in the Diocese, and recommendation as to amenities which it is reasonable to provide in schools.

CONCLUSION

The management of primary schools presents a number of problems all its own. The sheer numbers of such schools increases the difficulty of recruitment of managers in numerical terms, let alone quality. There is a strong case for arguing that some managers should be local people, just because they are local. However, in poor or run down areas this may well result in the appointment of managers with little or nothing to offer, and there may be nobody to give the Head any support or stimulus. It is, therefore, necessary to have a leavening of specialist members concerned with education, and we think that the colleges of education provide a most suitable and virtually untapped source. The Inner London Education Authority has for some time reserved a place on each managing body for a lecturer from a college of education. It is, perhaps, more appropriate to recruit specialists from colleges of education than from universities for this purpose. Their numbers and distribution should make it possible to provide suitable managers in many areas. The numbers of schools involved also results in the strain on the administration in terms of clerking and the preparation of agendas and minutes being often very considerable, even though, according to many chief education officers, primary schools make relatively few demands on the administrative machine. It might be thought that a fully developed system of managing bodies for individual schools or for small groups would be hardly justified by the results achieved. If this view is considered valid, a possible development would be to have grouped managing bodies serving from two to four schools, with individual managers assigned as visitors to each school. Links with secondary schools might be secured by overlapping membership, rather than through joint managing and governing bodies. The burden on the administration is not considered to be impossible, according to some large counties and county boroughs and, indeed, in the largest authority of all the system is felt to be well worth while. However, where local education authorities consider that it would strain the system too much to have all managing bodies clerked from the Office, they might wish to consider following the practice of many voluntary schools and nominate a manager as the clerk. This arrangement should be subject to the safeguard that all managing bodies should be visited by an Assistant Education Officer, or a Divisional Officer, at least once a year, and that copies of the agenda and minutes should be sent promptly to the Office. An alternative practice would be for the secretary of a secondary school to take over some of the clerk's functions, insofar as he could prepare papers, take follow-up action with the Authority, and in general look after matters of procedure, as already happens in one local education authority. This could be regarded as another consequence of devolving administrative functions on to individual secondary schools.

7 The Government of Independent, Direct Grant and Voluntary Aided Schools

So far school government has been considered in terms of the county school in its relationship to the local education authority. There are, however, other modes of school government which repay study because they exemplify other principles, because they influence thinking about the recasting of the typical local education authority system, and because they throw a different light on the relations between the layman and the professional. Independent schools illustrate school government and trusteeship divorced from local authority control, and shared control is seen in voluntary aided and, to a much lesser degree, in direct grant schools.

These modes of school government are virtually unexplored by students of educational administration and their inclusion is amply justified by their own intrinsic interest and importance. Indeed, this chapter adds a fresh dimension to the main course of this study. The original stimulus came from the appointment of the Public Schools Commission in 1965. Material was collected relating to Independent, Direct Grant and Voluntary Aided Schools and formed the basis of a memorandum of evidence submitted to the Newsom Committee. It is from this memorandum that material for this chapter has been drawn and even though it may be felt to sit uneasily with the rest of the book, so little has been done in this field that its inclusion was felt to be justified. Yet no claim can be made that all modes of school government have been studied, since no mention has been made of the management and government of Catholic and Church of England voluntary aided schools. This omission detracts seriously from the completeness of this study, but to remedy it would have demanded resources which were not available.

THE GOVERNMENT OF INDEPENDENT SCHOOLS

It is curious that the Public Schools Commission paid so little attention to the composition and functions of school governors and governing bodies. Any scheme of total or partial integration would depend for its success or otherwise on close collaboration between the governing bodies of individual schools and local education authorities. The Commission, however, did no more than recommend[1] that one-third of the governing body of any integrated school should be non-foundation governors under a scheme to be approved by the proposed Boarding Schools Corporation. They also commended the practice of delegating authority to headmasters and headmistresses of independent schools and suggested that integration might encourage a wider delegation of powers to the governing bodies and heads of maintained schools. Apart from this, however, little interest was shown in the machinery of school government or in the ways in which the governing bodies of independent schools actually worked.

The survey upon which this chapter is based was carried out through interviews with heads, chairmen and members of governing bodies and clerks to foundations of some 20 independent schools of widely differing characteristics. Some were totally independent foundations, others were run by foundations with other interests. Some were the concern of religious bodies, of City Companies, or even of family trusts. Among the schools studied were some generally considered as 'progressive', unorthodox or experimental; girls' schools, schools with radically minded heads, schools already having a working relationship with local education authorities and schools of ancient or new beginnings. The heads of most, but not all of the schools, were members of the Headmasters' Conference. It was not always possible to obtain three points of view on the same school, but the cumulative evidence from the three categories of respondent relates to similar, if not identical, situations.

[1] 1st Report: Vol. I, paras 313–15; and see also Vol. II, Appendix 10, pp. 280–1.

THE COMPOSITION OF GOVERNING BODIES

The legal status of governing bodies varies, for they can be established as educational charities, as private trusts, or as limited liability companies. The reasons for this variation in practice are frequently historical, but there is a tendency to supersede former deeds by the establishment of limited liability companies, as this status is considered to give governing bodies greater freedom to act in financial and administrative matters. Sometimes, as when a school is governed by a foundation or a City Company, it is possible to combine the advantages of both kinds of status, with the governing body itself registered as a charity, while the foundation functions as a limited liability company. The composition of governing bodies of independent schools varies greatly, from the completely closed as, for example, one in which the members are the 'Master Warden and commonalty of the . . . Company in the City of London' to another which is in theory open to any person regularly subscribing not less than one guinea per annum to the standing appeal from which the school derives its charitable income. Some governing bodies are highly pluralistic as, for example, one whose membership consists of:

  1 hereditary member
  3 ex-officio members (a Bishop, a Dean, and a Lord Lieutenant)
 10 representative governors appointed severally by
      the governors of a local charity
      the head and assistant masters
      the local Members of Parliament acting jointly
      universities and two other learned bodies
5–9 co-optative governors, to be appointed by the Trustees.

Most of the governing bodies studied, apart from those where membership is specifically confined to one source, have ample provision for the selection of individuals who are thought to have a distinctive contribution to make. It is common for the universities, especially Oxford and Cambridge, to nominate governors and, in one or two instances governors can be elected by, but not from, the teaching staff. Other sources are the Church of England or other religious denominations, learned societies and, in some instances, local education authorities. Even where the membership is confined to one body, such as a charitable foundation or a City Company, it may be enlarged through the appointment of a schools committee, often enjoying a wide measure of discretion. The average governing body in the independent sector has considerably more members than is common for a county secondary school, a count of half of HMC schools showing that the median membership lies between 18 and 19. On some governing bodies the chairmanship is restricted to, for example, a member of a City Company or a hereditary governor, but such a provision is rare.

Most independent schools have their own individual governing body, and this is commonly regarded as a cardinal principle. Some heads expressed themselves very strongly on this matter, and said that they would not in any circumstances contemplate going to a school which has a shared governing body. However, there are many examples of twin boys' and girls' schools sharing the same governors, and this is not considered unfortunate. Some heads of schools 'sharing' a foundation considered that they had certain advantages. The individual character of their schools was guaranteed by their having their own school committees, whilst the foundation guaranteed their financial position. Heads of schools governed by City Companies, however, sometimes thought that there was a danger of the schools being regarded as an appendage of the Company, and that there was relatively little interest in them as schools. But City Companies were invariably considered as extremely generous, and this compensated for the rather proprietary interest which some appeared to take on occasion. In practice the appointment of a powerful schools committee from the ranks of the parent body seems to be sufficient to ensure that the interests of the school were very much kept at heart. In schools forming a group within the same foundation, links were guaranteed, not only through overlapping membership of the school committee and the foundation, but also through the Clerk or Secretary, who customarily attended both sets of meetings. This was generally welcomed, as the Clerk was able to speak with authority on matters of finance and policy. Some Schemes provide for local education authorities to nominate representatives and such a link is generally welcomed, particularly where the authority is paying the fees of a substantial number of pupils. It is considered by many heads and other governors that such representatives are worth having, since they are usually powerful and influential members of the authority.

Most systems of recruiting governors are quite informal, and when vacancies occur governors look around, singly or collectively, for suitable candidates. One or two chairmen of governing bodies and some heads thought that this informality had great limitations: governors recruited through personal friendship might have little to offer, and it was embarrassing to turn down any proposed candidate, particularly if he had already been notified of his impending election. Another criticism is that far too many governorships are given to the eminent, without sufficient attention being paid to the services that might be expected.

Some heads and chairmen expressed themselves very forcefully on the elderliness of their governors. On the whole, governors could serve for as long as they pleased. Only one example of an upper age limit was found, this being the generous one of 75. There seems to be no way of getting rid of governors who are past their best without causing ill-feeling. One Foundation, however, had a rule that no governor may serve for more than eight years at a time, and this is thought to ensure a proper balance in turnover and continuity of membership. A difficulty in getting younger people of the right calibre was that they were frequently unable to spare the time to serve, especially if this involved work on a finance or a building committee.

There were mixed feelings about Old Boys as governors. It is, indeed, implicitly understood in some cases that Old Boy governors shall not be in the majority. But there is a tendency for local education authorities, universities and other appointing bodies to choose Old Boys of the school concerned as their representatives. The main charge against Old Boy governors was that they were too backward looking and too conservative: this was especially true of Old Boys' Associations which, in the view of some heads, were much inclined to look back with fondness on times past and to deplore changes. Old boy governors and sometimes other governors were said to take a too proprietary interest in schools on occasion, for example, by approaching Heads to see if they would admit sons of old boys irrespective of their suitability.

University representatives were welcomed, but heads did not regard it as necessary to have 'educational experts' as governors; they themselves were able to act in this capacity. There was also a universal feeling of relief at the absence of governors nominated on a party political basis which was thought to be the bane of local authority schools.

Where there is provision for the teaching staff to appoint a governor it is often customary for them to choose a serving governor as their spokesman, and it is then entirely up to this governor to decide how he executes his functions. Instances were cited of such staff appointees spending the evening before a governors' meeting in the Common Room, so as to acquaint themselves with the views of the staff in the absence of the head. It is customary for Heads to have the right to attend the Governors' meeting, although occasionally the HMA has had to draw the attention of foundations to the desirability of maintaining this principle, both to avoid diminishing the status of the Head, and to enable him to contribute to decisions which he will have to execute. Indeed it can be argued that the Head's involvement in the governing body should go further than this, and should include membership of house and other appropriate committees.

The internal organization of governing bodies varies very greatly. Most of the larger governing bodies have an executive committee, generally consisting of from five to ten members, and there are often other committees for buildings and finance. One or two heads thought their governing bodies were too large, and that there were too many meetings: this is particularly the case where the school is a subordinate part of a foundation. One head claimed that he had to attend meetings of the governing body every month, with meetings of the executive committee in between, although there was really only sufficient business for one meeting of the committee and one meeting of the governing body each term. Meetings were very pleasant social occasions, but tended to degenerate into gossip. The governors thought that they were in close touch with the school because they met so often, but this was far from being the case.

THE APPOINTMENT OF HEADMASTERS

Various stipulations relating to the appointment of heads are found in the schemes governing independent schools. The actual procedure however is reserved to the governing body. Generally it is required that a vacancy should be advertised and, in most Public Schools, it is laid down that the post is open to graduates of British or Commonwealth universities. Occasionally, also the head is required to be a member of the Church of England. There is a standard clause to the effect that the Head

shall not hold any office or appointment which, in the opinion of the Trustees, may interfere with the proper performance of his duties . . . or have any benefice having the cure of souls.

The appointment of a head is naturally regarded by governors as their most important single function. A sub-committee is invariably set up to draw up a short list and make initial soundings. Likely candidates may be approached privately by members of the governing body to whom they are known; their names may be sent in by an Oxford or Cambridge college with an interest in the school; and replies to advertisements, where these are used, produce other applicants. Once the short-list is made interviewing may take many forms, ranging from the informal discussion to the set interview. Sometimes, the applicants may be asked to bring their wives with them. Whatever procedures are used, the governors consulted claimed with virtual unanimity that they knew how to choose a good head: but they also felt that their predecessors had not always had the same talent.

The procedure for dismissal is standard in almost all cases. The appointment can be terminated, with six months' notice, at the governors' pleasure. In urgent cases dismissal may be confirmed at a second meeting at which the dismissal has been proposed, provided that such dismissal is confirmed by a two-thirds majority of those present and voting. The head is commonly allowed to make a personal representation, accompanied by a friend. In practice 'at pleasure' is a phrase not interpreted in a capricious or arbitrary manner. It is recognized by Heads that the body which appointed them must retain the ultimate right, subject to appropriate safeguards, and generally to compensation, of terminating their appointment: but antique turns of phrase in articles of government do not take priority over contracts of service.

Pressure for dismissal will spring from a progressive feeling of unease; if this is not allayed, the first step will be for the chairman to inform the Head privately that he will have to go; if the Head is unresponsive the chairman will indicate that the next meeting of the governing body may call for his resignation; and only if the Head is unwilling to oblige will the formal machinery for dismissal be put in motion. Put like this, there seems little difference between the position of independent and maintained schools; but certainly the informal pressures, and the knowledge that the governing body can in the last resort dismiss a Head if due procedures are followed, form significant differences. As in the maintained sector, the Headmasters Association will do what it can to protect the interests of its members, advising Heads for example not to offer their formal resignation until fair and adequate terms have been agreed.

Recourse to formal institutional machinery in the appointment and dismissal of heads is by no means the rule. Trials of strength and the taking up of entrenched positions are rarely met with, in comparison to the situation obtaining in maintained schools. Other resources are available to governors: for example, a governing body can easily make a head's life intolerable, either by refusing to give him anything he asks for, or by taking too close an interest in the school for his comfort. In these circumstances a head will probably not wish to stand on such rights as he enjoys, but will prefer to move on elsewhere. In one foundation the position of heads was described as being very much like that of football club managers. Indeed five heads had been dismissed within nine years, on account of the dissatisfaction governors had felt with the management of their schools.

OTHER APPOINTMENTS

For assistant masters the standard model provides for them to be appointed to the service of the governing body. Thus, even where it is laid down that the head has powers to dismiss staff without reference to the governors, he carries out such action as their agent. There are two variants: in one, an assistant master is appointed by and holds office at the pleasure of the head, but his dismissal is referred to the governing body who may require a written report from the head; in the other, an assistant master serves a probationary period not exceeding three terms, during which period the head may dismiss him without consulting the governing body. At one school, there is an astounding practice of regarding all assistant masters as being on probation again following the appointment of a new head.

In some schools there is pressure for written contracts of service, but for the most part relationships between heads and assistant masters are regarded as being governed by gentlemen's agreements and by custom and use. Little reference was made in interviews to enlisting the help of teachers' associations, although their standing in certain matters is becoming increasingly recognized. While there are relatively few AMA members in independent schools, where a member is in dispute with his Head, and more particularly if he thinks that he is at risk of unfair dismissal, the officers of the two associations may well consider the issue together and produce a joint recommendation to the interested parties. Such joint action is made easier to achieve as the associations share the same premises.

There are, of course, considerable statutory limitations on the appointment, dismissal and conditions of service of both heads and assistants. Safeguards are provided in the Contracts of Employment Act, 1963, and the Industrial Relations Act 1971. In addition, the Associations concerned have taken their own steps to establish standards and procedures; for example, the Governing Bodies Association has issued circulars on relations between heads and governors and upon conditions of service and terms of appointment. The teachers' associations are always ready to advise their members about any draft contract submitted to them for signature and are frequently able to suggest amendments acceptable to both parties on such matters as tenure, notice, superannuation, holiday entitlement or financial responsibility. Such amendments may appear trivial at the time, but can avert later difficulties.

In general, however, the parties involved in the government of independent schools do not rely greatly on formal undertakings, and the effect of the two Acts mentioned is felt more indirectly, in the influence they exert on governing bodies and heads to act according to their spirit rather than their letter. If governing bodies and heads are less inclined now to act in an arbitrary fashion, this may be due less to the possibility of sanctions, pressure on them to conform to standard procedures and a desire to avoid antagonizing teachers' associations, and more to a shortage of teachers and the interest of governors and heads in keeping a reasonably contented staff.

RESPONSIBILITIES OF HEADS AND GOVERNORS

The relative jurisdiction of the governors and head over the management is commonly stated in terms similar to those found in Articles of Government for county secondary schools, the standard clauses being:

The governors shall prescribe the general subjects of instruction, the relative prominence and value to be assigned to each group of subjects, when reports shall be required to be made to them by the head, arrangements respecting holidays, school terms, etc. . . . and they shall fix the amount which they think proper to be paid out of the income of the foundation for providing and maintaining the proper school plant and apparatus, and awarding prizes.

The head's responsibilities are as follows:

The head shall determine, subject to the approval of the governors, in what proportion the sums fixed by the governors for maintenance and school plant and apparatus and prizes shall be divided among the various objects for which it is fixed in the aggregate, and the governors shall pay the sum through the hands of the head, or as they think best.

The head is also generally responsible for

. . . the choice of books, methods of teaching, the arrangement of classes and school hours, and generally the whole organization and management and discipline of the school, including the power of expelling boys from the school.

These responsibilities are further specified in some Deeds of Trust, where it is laid down that

Instruction shall be given in the school in such subjects proper to be taught in a public secondary school for boys, as the head, in consultation with the Trustees, shall from time to time determine: subject to the provisions of the Scheme, the course of instruction shall be according to the classification made by the head.

Clauses such as these leave governors and head a very wide scope for determining the general educational character of a school. In only two cases studied do Deeds or Schemes contain any mention of the educational character of the school or of its curriculum. In one it is laid down that

The school shall provide a sound practical liberal education suitable for boys who are intended for commercial and similar occupations.

The subjects to be studied are: religious instruction, mathematics, Latin, English, modern languages, writing, arithmetic, the elements of science, history and geography. Within this framework, the head has entire control of what is taught, but it is a control that is limited by the requirement that all boys should study mathematics throughout their school life and science and modern languages for at least nine consecutive terms. These articles were made in 1824, and still stand today.

This apparent lack of definition of the educational character of long-established schools reflects the determination of the nineteenth-century reformers to free endowed schools from the restrictions imposed on them by early Schemes. Together with the omission of any reference of the age-range to be catered for and of any stated objectives (e.g. that the school should prepare boys for entry to the universities and the learned professions) the result is that governing bodies have the power, should they so wish, to transform the educational character of their schools. It is important to note, however, in view of proposals that have been made to integrate independent schools within the main school structure, that Schemes generally lay down that there shall be an entrance examination, under the direction of the head in consultation with the governing body. No mention is made of the standard of this examination, nor of the subjects which it should include, but its existence clearly provides for whatever degree of selectiveness is acceptable to head and governors.

FINANCE AND BUILDINGS

Several governors interviewed drew a parallel between governing bodies and Boards of Directors. Their own function was to appoint a head whose position they regarded as similar to that of a managing director, and thereafter to concern themselves with financial matters of chronic urgency. There is often a constant struggle to keep a school above water. Endowments which were ample before the war are quite inadequate now. The difficulties of improving facilities and keeping good staff, whilst at the same time not pricing the school out of the market are very great. Consequently much depends on the business acumen either of individual governors or of the Bursar or Clerk. Governing bodies are concerned to seek fresh sources of finance to supplement existing endowments and fee income, and more specifically to provide capital for new building schemes. They do this partly by appealing to parents and other well-wishers for help through donations or preferably covenants; by approaching interested bodies such as educational trusts or industrial organizations; and by making use of their own personal and professional contacts with the world of finance.

Some of the governors' financial activities impinge directly on the internal organization of the school, for example if they propose to institute central feeding instead of separate catering by houses. A major change of this nature is acceptable; but clashes can occur where discretion in financial matters is possessed by heads or housemasters. A case was reported in one school of a housemaster who spent much more on food for his boys than was customary. The governors repeatedly asked him to economize, but he remained adamant on the ground that his first duty was towards the boys. Ultimately, the governors decided they would have to surcharge him if he persisted, and he was notified that the matter would be discussed officially at their next meeting. The housemaster resigned his house just in time to avoid a surcharge. Similarly, while heads exercise control over admission standards, this professional function has clear financial implications. If they wish to improve their school's level of academic attainment by raising the standards of entry, they run a risk of reducing their intake and, accordingly, their fees—the most important source of revenue income. In considering such a change of admissions policy, governors will feel a need to work out the full financial consequences, and to ensure that the Head is made fully aware of them when operating his new policy.

Headmasters and bursars are allowed a great deal of discretion in interpreting the decisions or views of their governing body. The average governing body meets only once a term, with the finance committee probably meeting a few weeks earlier. There is certainly no close day to day control, even where a governing body consists mainly of local figures. An interesting example of such discretion appeared at one school where the governors had refused to sanction a proposed increase in fees to help buy land for a proposed extension. The head then took it on himself to send a letter to every parent asking if they would contribute towards a fund for the acquisition of further property in the neighbourhood. This got a very good response, and the head's initiative was applauded by the governors.

The part played by the governors in determining salary structure inside schools is ill-defined, and generalizations are impossible. Indeed, on occasion it appeared doubtful whether there were any salary scales in any real sense. At one school it was stated that newly appointed assistant masters had not been told what salary they would receive, thereby confirming the hypothesis that talk about money in independent schools is 'not the done thing'. This is claimed to be the case in John Wilson's amusing *Public Schools and Private Practice*, 1962. He writes (p. 94):

I know a man who worked for many years in a school without any kind of contract or agreement on either side. Occasional and curious things happened to his salary: at one stage he found himself with a £50 expense account for expenditure entailed as a housemaster (though actually one spends rather over £100 a year on one's house), and once with his salary cheque a note arrived from the headmaster saying, 'I am giving you an extra £50 for being good'. (I give the exact words). Certainly he had no cause to complain, but the insecurity involved might have disturbed an older man. This sort of thing is a symptom of the necessity for the financial authorities having a free hand. Similarly, there are members of the staff who are in effect bribed to stay: and others who by a sparing financial hand-out are encouraged to go. All this is done without open discussion, because that would not be nice; but there is a kind of underground realism about money in the public schools, nevertheless.

Some schools have their own salary scales: in one there are large increments in the first years, which are then gradually tapered off. This is intended to act as an incentive to assistant masters to seek posts elsewhere if they have not been promoted as housemasters, and it is said to be very effective. If those interviewed report typical situations, it would appear unheard of for any headmaster to refer the case of any individual assistant's salary to the governors for decision.

There seems to be no fixed practice in granting special allowances, although extra payments for living-in and the provision of
accommodation outside the school may be thought of as equivalent benefits. Some governing bodies have encouraged the practice
of setting a limit, generally 15 years, for a housemaster's tenure of
office.

The relationship between head and bursar is of paramount
importance for decision-making in the school and by the governing body. A principle often enunciated is that the bursar should be
responsible to the governing body through the head, but this
principle can be interpreted in many different ways. Clearly it
matters very greatly whether the head is expected to have any
financial expertise, or whether this is regarded entirely as the
bursar's province, so that he is in a position to tell the head what
he can have.

In one school the head and the bursar were regarded by the
governors as being nominally equal, with the bursar responsible
for finance and the head for academic matters. In other schools
heads undertook a great deal of financial administration on their
own, leaving the bursar a very subordinate role. Usually governing bodies are careful to pay regard to the head's wishes when
appointing bursars and similar staff, and often the head will be a
member of the appointing committee. However, heads cannot
always count on being consulted, and sometimes governors take a
view of their responsibilities which is unacceptable to heads. The
Board of one foundation decided to dismiss a deputy bursar after
one year's service. For this purpose they held a private business
meeting, excluding the head, and informed him only after the
decision had been taken. This led to a showdown, in which the
head said very firmly that he would have expected the governors
to ask for his views on their proposed action. He also indicated
that he would not stand for a similar lack of consultation in the
future.

There are, it would seem, almost as many conceptions of the
role of bursar as there are foundations. A bursar may act addi-
tionally as clerk to the governing body (although some heads and

governors think this puts him in an impossible position) and may have responsibility for the appointment of non-teaching staff. Frequently he enjoys direct access to the governing body, and he may also have a very free hand in the school's financial administration, for example in negotiating with local education authorities, or in dealing with parents who do not pay fees promptly. He will also play an important part in the promotion of appeals and the administration of covenanting schemes.

Even where a bursar is not clerk to the governing body he may well be regarded in practice as the governors' watchdog. He has a strong position as the governors' de facto financial and sometimes legal advisor. Bursars have their own professional association, unlike clerks to governors of independent schools, and thus enjoy an effective means of reducing the professional isolation in which they work. A regular flow of bulletins is produced on such matters as the effect of the introduction of new taxes or the implications of new changes in company law, and this information service is clearly indispensible for the effective financial management of schools.

After general finance, the governors' main executive functions centre round buildings and other school properties. They have to find the money for maintenance, repairs and extensions, and are also responsible for letting contracts and finding architects. Most governing bodies have a Buildings Sub-Committee on which any governor with the right kind of industrial or other experience will be expected to serve. At times this committee will meet more frequently than the governing body, particularly during planning and building operations. Here again the bursar, as the man on the spot, may assume responsibilities as the governors' agent and negotiate with sub-contractors.

Several heads and governors felt that it was a great advantage to be able to plan and carry through a long-term development programme without it being subject to cuts at the behest of a local authority Finance Committee tied to annual budgeting and to annual variations in the rates. But some heads were very much aware of the possibility of long-term commitments inhibiting developments desirable for the teaching and life of the school, because existing resources were already earmarked.

CURRICULUM AND ORGANIZATION

The immediate reaction of both governors and heads, when challenged, is that curriculum and internal organization are entirely the province of the head; and that, while the head has a duty to give the governors some idea of what is going on, they should not challenge his actions or seek to bring pressure to bear on him in respect of such matters. This is an over-simplification. There is ample evidence of governors' concern with the life and work of their schools, and of the extent to which some heads are inhibited from making changes because of their estimate of their governors' reactions.

Most heads present written reports to their governors either every term or once a year before Speech Day. These reports can be substantial documents, often running into 20 pages or more, and many refer to every aspect of the school's activities. They deal with staff appointments, academic and athletic results, and new developments of note. They also provide the head with an opportunity for discussing matters of more general interest, such as the future of independent schools or changes in VI form courses. The interest shown by governors seems to vary from the keen to the perfunctory. Governors sometimes suggest that changes should be considered: for example, the introduction of a Business Studies course or of a less frequently taught language, such as Russian. A head who considers such enthusiasms misplaced can generally produce good reasons for seeing that nothing is done. At the same time, most seem to welcome interest in academic matters provided that their own responsibilities are left clear. Indeed, in some cases, heads had proposed that their governors should set up education committees to inform themselves in more detail of the work of the school, and thus be in a position to consider proposals put to them with a degree of competent interest. A particularly notable instance of governors' increasing concern with curriculum development has been their interest in science teaching and laboratory provision, which arose from the establishment of the Industrial Fund in the mid-1950s. This Fund, it will be remembered, was set up to match, and probably surpassed, the special extra provision being made by DES for maintained secondary schools at that time.

Governors, of course, concern themselves with major questions of organization as, for example, whether a school should broaden its intake to bring in less academic pupils, whether a larger number of places should be offered to a local education authority, or whether a day-boy element should be enlarged. One head of a small school supported by a local family trust felt that 'he could almost get away with murder', particularly if he could present controversial developments as purely technical issues. He had had a struggle, however, over the proposed introduction of a House system. The governors held strongly that the school's character as laid down in the trust deed made the head's direct responsibility for all pastoral care paramount, and had opposed setting up any system which would lessen such responsibility. It needed a great deal of firm argument and persuasion to convince the governors that the increasing size of the school made it necessary for the head reluctantly to delegate some of his pastoral duties.

ATTITUDES TO INNOVATION

There are other indications which support the view that heads have to be circumspect in their dealings with their governors, especially when it is a matter of changing some old-established custom. One head wanted to replace shorts by grey flannel trousers, as he found that the older boys felt ridiculous in what they, and he, considered very out-of-date garb. However, bare knees were one of the traditions of this school, and the head had had to bide his time before the governors would even consider discussing the proposed change. Similarly, heads who proposed to abolish fagging or corporal punishment, or substitute some form of local voluntary service for CCF activities said that they would certainly sound out the governors first, even if it was only to tell them what they intended to do. It was frequently found that though governors, especially Old Boys, might make a great show of protesting against proposed changes, they were quite often reconciled to them within a year and soon forgot what the fuss was about.

These relatively trivial instances do serve to illustrate the general tenor of head-governor relationships, at least as seen by heads. The prevailing view is that the governors had known what the views and attitudes of a head were when they appointed him. It was, then, to be expected that the head should feel free to act within his own sphere, which comprised everything bearing on the work and life of the school. But, even the most experimentally-minded heads thought that they had a duty to be aware of the school's general traditions and to remember that, while the school was likely to be there indefinitely, they themselves would retire sooner or later.

The first innovatory step was often the hardest. Once the governors had got used to the idea that change was natural and desirable, the pace could be rapid. One head said that his governors had consented to his first major innovation by giving the Clerk instructions to record their agreement *nemine contradicente*, instead of giving it their unanimous support. They had also required an assurance that no cost would fall on the foundation and called for a progress report at the end of the year. A few years later they were all most enthusiastic over the success of this particular experiment, and subsequent changes had been introduced much more easily.

Some heads found it expedient to bring up tentative proposals before the governors so that they could have the satisfaction of debating them and turning them down. It is, indeed, accepted that the rejection of a proposal by a head is not necessarily a mark of lack of confidence. Heads were reconciled to occasional defeats. One had proposed opening a school shop, but governors representing local interests argued that this would subject local tradesmen to unfair competition, and that they could not support it. The head had decided to take the matter no further. If a head was really serious about a proposal, he would work on the governors over a period of time, and would certainly get the chairman and other key members of the governing body on his side first.

An example of a kind of interest frequently displayed by governors in their school was given by a chairman of very long standing and considerable national eminence. He made it a practice to spend one or two weekends at the school each term and had remarked more than once on the small number attending Evensong and on the length of boys' hair. The head had pointed out that he had thought it proper to abolish compulsory Chapel except for one Sunday service, as it was both unreasonable and self-defeating to compel boys to take part in religious observance, when they should be encouraged to solve their own ethical and spiritual problems in their own way. He agreed that some boys grew their hair too long, but thought that their morale would suffer if compulsory shearing was decreed. Simple repression would be resented all round and might lead to much more obviously undesirable signs of teenage independence or rebelliousness. He therefore proposed to leave it to the prefects to take action in the most extreme cases, and in this way the chairman was persuaded that something was being done. The point of interest here is that the head thought it worthwhile giving a full and reasoned explanation to his chairman and regarded the chairman's interest in a matter of internal discipline as quite legitimate. Similarly, the chairman was satisfied, having raised these matters informally that the head would go as far as he could to meet him. Neither party considered taking up a stronger position; the head might, for example, have claimed that the issue was one for him alone, and in this event the chairman might have decided to express his concern formally at a subsequent governors' meeting. But there was no attempt from either side to argue from defined rights and duties.

In form the government of independent schools has changed little over the past hundred years. The crucial relationship, that of a head and his governors still depends upon an intricate pattern of shared values and assumptions expressed, if at all, in commonplace clichés. Governors of independent schools come from the same social groupings as the boys and girls in their schools; they have had the same kind of school and home experience; and they have the same assumptions regarding their role as the heads themselves, namely, they respect the autonomy of the head within the school. Nevertheless, all parties have, individually and collectively, a very sensitive awareness of what is expected of them and how far they can go. Both heads and governors expect that they will share a considerable consensus of opinion about what is best for the school and that this consensus will be sufficient to resolve most differences. As long as this consensus persists, it is rare for differences to lead to anything like a show-down. But once it no longer exists, a head will probably decide that his future lies elsewhere. The governors, in an independent school, hold all the cards and there is no bureaucratic structure which protects the office-holder such as exists in the maintained schools sector. On the other hand, the governors themselves, unlike councillors or education officers, are solely responsible for their school and success and security depends for them also, not on devising and implementing policies, but in their school's standing and achievements.

DIRECT GRANT AND AIDED GRAMMAR SCHOOLS

Articles of government for direct grant schools and aided grammar schools are made for individual schools or for schools grouped under a foundation, by the Secretary of State for Education and Science or the Charity Commissioners acting on his behalf. The most important provisions follow closely those already met in respect of independent schools: for example, the schemes for one group of direct grant schools gives the governors exactly the same powers as are possessed by the governors of independent schools. Similarly, the standard articles for aided grammar schools provide that

subject to the provisions of the development plan approved for the area by the Minister as to the general educational character of the schools and their place in the educational system, the governors shall have the general direction of the conduct and curriculum of the schools.

The interpretation of this clause has not been tested in the courts, and it is impossible to anticipate the consequences of a head-on clash between the governors and the local authority responsible for the development plan. On the face of it, however, it appears clear that a substantial degree of responsibility rests with the governors, particularly since it is not clear whether the reference to the 'educational system' refers to the system in operation in any one individual authority or to more.

The admission of pupils to direct grant schools is entirely in the hands of the head, with certain reserve powers given to governors. In aided grammar schools it is a matter for agreement between the governors and the local education authority, who are to take into account the wishes of the parents, any school records and other information which may be available, the general type of education most suited for a particular child and the views of the headmaster or headmistress. In addition, the local education authority is to determine which candidates are qualified for admission by reason of their having reached a sufficient educational standard. The parallel clause in the articles of voluntary controlled schools some years ago formed the subject of a High Court judgement in the Enfield Grammar School case discussed elsewhere (Ch. 3, pp. 60–63). The judgement has been interpreted as meaning that the articles do not permit the local education authority to abolish specific educational qualifications for admission into selective schools.

The governors' control over the character of individual schools is as broad and as general in direct grant schools and aided grammar schools as in independent schools. For example, the articles of one aided grammar school merely states

there shall be two schools of the foundation, that is to say a school for boys, to be called '. . . Grammar School', and a school for girls, to be called '. . . High School for Girls'

The clerk of the governing body is appointed by the governors in direct grant schools, and by the governors in consultation with the local education authority in aided grammar schools. This provision means that each governing body has a very complete control of its own affairs.

In both direct grant schools and aided grammar schools all the teaching staff are employed by the governors. They are also appointed by the governors subject, in the case of aided grammar schools, to the consent of the local education authority and to various safeguards to ensure that the headmaster and other staff have necessary educational qualifications.

As regards financial matters, a local education authority has no part in the affairs of a direct grant school. In respect of an aided grammar school it may protest to the Department of Education and Science that it does not think that certain proposed expenditure is wise, but it is for the governors and the Department to take a decision. The principle of direct access to the Department is a very effective means of safeguarding the independence of aided grammar schools from local education authority proposals.

THE ROLE OF THE CLERK

The importance of the Clerk to the governors of direct grant and aided grammar schools cannot be overstressed, as many heads, governors and education officers have acknowledged. He is the key figure in communication between the head and the foundation. As one head put it, the Clerk has a mastery of financial detail which many governors cannot be expected to possess. He may well be in daily contact with the head and play a decisive part in negotiating on major policy issues with the Department of Education and Science and local education authorities, leaving the head free to deal with educational matters and school routine. One Clerk thought it important to preserve the principle of administrator talking to administrator, as heads might be unaware of the wider implications of action taken on behalf of their own school.

In foundations concerned with more than one school, Clerks have to take care to hold a balance between the schools, and in the view of some heads this requires qualities of fairness, tact and trust. As one head put it: 'A request for an unusual item for one school entailing abnormal expenditure invariably prompts emotional and irrational reactions from the kind of governor who wants to preserve "parity" for both schools.' The chairman, of course, has an important part to play in this kind of situation, but since contact between heads and Clerks is more constant relations between them are especially important.

The difficulties which may arise on a dual foundation are set out in admirable detail in the following contribution from a headmaster in his reply to the national survey of heads; on a multiple foundation the problems may well be even greater.

The foundation comprises separate boys' and girls' schools. The two schools share the same governing body and both heads attend the same meetings. While it may be an advantage to share common problems in conference—for instance, the headmaster covers the requirement of playing fields, the headmistress of the kitchen—and sit back occasionally to observe 'how the other half lives', there are snags.

(1) Governors' meetings are enormously protracted by dealing with two reports, two sets of problems—so that some important business is hastily concluded.

(2) Women governors particularly fail to recognise the volume of correspondence which falls on a boys' school from would-be employers, career sponsors, follow-up of recent old boys' job-hunting or job changing after university, participation of headmasters in conferences or on committees (we get together more often than headmistresses), and are reluctant to approve adequate office staff for this purpose.

(3) Invidious comparisons are made at the annual review of GCE results (both schools being well above average for their respective and different Boards), through a failure, even on the part of academic governors, to appreciate that the two schools, with their approval, organise their curricula differently. To avoid this sort of rivalry, my colleague and I have to resist—and our sympathy is such that we have no difficulty in resisting—the temptation to beat drums.

(4) Unless the more influential and perceptive governors on a dual foundation study accounts closely, and observe the provisions of the instrument of government meticulously, there is a tendency for adminis-

tration to tidy up accounts by setting the surplus of one school to offset the shortfall of the other. This can only be countered by an untimely spending spree.

(5) A good teacher does not take together two parallel forms, nor does he give exactly the same lesson to the two classes separately. Nor does the doctor, solicitor or accountant double up his patients or clients. Governors, busy people though they are, should not yield to the attraction of dealing at one sitting with the education of 800 (or 1200/1600) pupils when they could bring their combined expertise and human qualities to contribute more effectively to the welfare of 400 in two (or three/four) sittings.

RELATIONS OF DIRECT GRANT SCHOOLS AND AIDED GRAMMAR SCHOOLS WITH LOCAL EDUCATION AUTHORITIES

The main guarantee of the independence of direct grant and aided grammar schools resides in the statutory provisions which stipulate that one-third only of the membership of their governing bodies are to be representatives of local education authorities, the majority being appointed by the foundation. This ensures that governing bodies have a majority of independent members and are thus in a position very close to that of governing bodies of independent schools.

But, in addition, most direct grant schools and aided grammar schools are leading schools in the area from which they draw their pupils and many, though not all, have long and distinguished histories. They have been used to respectful handling by local education authorities, which have looked to them to provide a substantial number of selective school places. They are also very conscious of their status and of their degree of financial independence. With well endowed schools especially there is an awareness that a foundation could in the last resort turn the schools it controls into independent establishments and thus remove them entirely from the local orbit. As the chairman of the governing body of one well-placed aided grammar school put it

We are in the position of an assistant master with a substantial private income. We can stand up to the head and need not fear the possible consequences if he wanted to get rid of us.

Foundations of such schools are thus often able to drive a hard bargain with local education authorities, and in this connexion their direct access to the Department of Education and Science is of major significance. Where the foundation and a local education authority have not been able to resolve a difference, the views of the former not infrequently prevail with the Department.

Many local education authorities are prepared to do much to keep the goodwill of direct grant and aided grammar schools, not simply because of the help they can give in providing extra school places, but because of their place in the life of a town or county area. There is keen competition among councillors and members of education committees to serve as local authority representatives on their governing bodies, and they are welcomed by foundation members for being able to put the school's case in the right quarters. Party differences do not appear to obtrude themselves on the governing bodies of direct grant and aided grammar schools, even over such matters as secondary school reorganization. Foundation members are always in a sufficient preponderance to ensure that they do not encroach upon the prescribed functions of governing bodies. This suggests that fears expressed by heads and governors of independent schools that 'integration' would bring party politics into their schools' affairs is misplaced or exaggerated. One head of an aided grammar school in a highly 'political' area said:

The chairman is a councillor of long standing who has been in the past leader of a strong Labour party on the local council. The vice-chairman is an Old Boy of the school and a strong Conservative. The chairman and vice-chairman work very well indeed together . . . Approximately half our governing body are actually on the local education divisional executive. Some of them give me very valuable personal advice and support, particularly the chairman and vice-chairman, and as well as they have their finger on the pulse pretty well . . . We have not been bedevilled on our governing body by politics—on the contrary, over the years we have been remarkably free of it.

Within the administrative context the control that local educa-tion authorities can exercise over aided grammar schools is limited. It is true that a standard provision in articles of government re-quires that governors should furnish the local education authority with such returns and reports as the latter may require. This is interpreted in terms of attendance and other data and is certainly not seen either by local education authorities or by the schools as means by which an authority can exercise close surveillance. In addition it is usual for governing bodies and local education authorities to send each other copies of the agenda and minutes of their meetings. But most communication of real significance is that undertaken on a day-to-day basis by the head, as agent of the governors and the education officers of the authority: in some cases the clerk to the governors also takes an active part.

There is an important provision in the standard articles which indicates a major difference between the status of aided grammar schools and county secondary schools. In the former consultation between head and chairman of governors is stipulated on matters affecting the welfare of the school; in the latter, the chief educa-tion officer is also accorded a place. Moreover, in the case of aided grammar schools, a chief education officer has no right to attend meetings of governors except when a headmaster is to be ap-pointed. On other occasions he may attend by invitation only, and in practice this is confined to such exceptional circumstances as the preparation of an authority's development plan, or its pro-posals for secondary reorganization.

Governors of an aided school have effective powers, subject to consultation with the local education authority on matters relating to educational standards and the qualifications of teaching staff; and of course, to compliance with staffing ratios. Working rela-tionships with local education authorities seem to be generally good and heads, governors and clerks to governing bodies have emphasized that this is the case, even when such potentially explosive issues as that of secondary school reorganization are being discussed. In part this may be due to the awareness of local education authorities of the potential independence of many aided schools; in part, also, it may be due to the considerable influence which the representatives of an authority on a school's governing body are able to exert.

The pattern of government of independent schools, direct grant schools and aided schools follows closely, in its essentials, that laid down in the middle of the last century. It is a pattern that has been only partially successful when adopted within the maintained schools sector. Its essential feature is that it entrusts a school or a group of schools to the care of a small group of individuals, or foundation governors, who ensure continuity and who are in ultimate control of the property and financial resources of the school or schools. In maintained schools the position is quite different in these two respects. Responsiveness to local opinion, rather than continuity and dependence on a parent body for all finance means that the responsibility borne by managers and governors for their schools is only very partial. It remains to be considered in what ways their role can and should be re-defined.

8 Governing Bodies and the Administration of Education

THE PRESENT SITUATION

In the memorandum of evidence submitted to the Royal Commission on Local Government the present situation in school government was summarized as follows:

There are many authorities, especially county boroughs, in which managing and governing bodies are mere formalities and are accorded only a minimal role within strong and highly burcaucratised structures. In such authorities schools are grouped together in large numbers, the business transacted by governing bodies is confined to minor routine matters, their membership is restricted as closely as possible to members of the council or of the education committee itself, and officers and teachers tend to settle the affairs of individual schools with as little reference as possible to lay members of the authority.

There is a fairly substantial number of authorities, both counties and county boroughs, in which managers and governors, serving single schools or small groups of schools, perform a number of functions, but in which there is substantial uncertainty and frustration concerning their role. In such authorities much depends upon the experience and personal authority of individual education officers, heads and governors, upon changes in political fortunes, and upon status differences between the schools concerned. In such authorities the attendance of governors at school functions is often perfunctory and little or no interest is shown by them in visiting and getting to know their schools.

There is a minority of authorities, mainly counties, in which the place of managers and governors is more or less accepted, in which they perform essential functions within the local authority framework, and in which there is a predisposition in favour of their responsibilities being increased. In such authorities governors, in particular, have a decisive role to play in the interviewing of applicants for senior posts, their requests concerning buildings and equipment carry weight, close attention is paid to their views on matters of policy affecting their schools, and the clerking of their meetings is regarded as a matter of some importance. In such authorities heads and chairmen of governors develop and are encouraged to develop close and positive relationships.[1]

It was argued that variations in the form and functions of managers and governors reflected:

(a) *The county—county borough division*. The municipal form of local government favours close control of schools by officers acting for elected representatives; on the other hand, the county style of government favours a dispersal of control, owing to geographical factors and the existence, within a county, of areas, both rural and urban, possessing their own distinctive characteristics. In the first case, then, governing bodies are not felt to be administrative necessities and can, indeed, be seen as a potential and dangerous threat to the unity of control exercised by the Committee and its officers; in the second case they can be, and are, means by which the county administration can draw support from local people in towns and rural areas that are conscious of their own identity.

(b) *Size of authority*. Size of authority in itself does not constitute a decisive factor. In the counties its influence, and the assessment of its influence, is blurred by the existence, in many though not all areas, of Excepted Districts and Divisional Executives. No generalisation can be made about large county boroughs; in two cases as least governing bodies have a part to play in administrative matters and exert some general influence; in others their significance is slight. Some, though not all, of the medium-sized and smaller county boroughs present a picture of control by officers and committee members.

(c) *Social and Economic Status*. The respect in which a managing or governing body is held by heads and officers depends on the extent to which it consists of men and women who are educationally and socially their equals or who are keenly interested in the school and in the population that it serves.

In any given area, there appears to be a marked tendency for service

[1] Royal Commission on Local Government in England. Research Studies 6. *School Management and Government*, by George Baron and D. A. Howell, H.M.S.O. 1968, pp. 139–40.

with highly regarded schools, particularly grammar schools and large comprehensive schools, to attract and secure the services of leading councillors and of men and women of relatively high qualifications.

(d) *Political Party Influences*. The hypothesis can be advanced that where party divisions are clearly marked and councils and committees are divided on wholly political lines no real responsibilities are accorded to managing and governing bodies. This is not wholly true and there are striking instances to the contrary. Political party influence, however, correlates highly with population concentrations and the municipal form of government, of which it is one aspect. It is especially noticeable in some authorities in which the Labour Party holds control or has become established as an effective political party.

(e) *History and tradition*. There is much to suggest that the place accorded to managing and governing bodies results from less apparent factors than those discussed. The attention paid to the individual school in London, for example, reflects the early detailed system of school management characteristic of the London School Board; the concern of the Education Committee and officers in one large city that no other agency should stand between them and the schools, on the other hand, reflects or at least is in line with the policy of the first Director of Education of that city. There are indications in other authorities that practice still reflects the policy adopted at a formative stage in the past, as the result of the emergence of a strong local personality. There would seem to be clear need for full awareness of local conditions when reforms in systems of school management and government are contemplated.[2]

In considering the frequent ineffectiveness of managers and governors, it is necessary to see them within the total context of the local administration of education.

MANAGERS AND GOVERNORS IN THE POWER STRUCTURE OF EDUCATION

The position of managers and governors of county schools, whether primary or secondary, differs fundamentally from that of

[2] ibid., pp. 140-1.

governors of independent, direct grant and voluntary aided schools. The latter are ultimately responsible for the continuance of their school, at least in the form in which it exists. They have ultimate responsibility for buildings, equipment and staffing and they are not accountable to public or representative bodies. The case of county schools is quite different. For them it is the local education authority which is, and must be, the controlling agency, responsible to the community and its elected representatives, for the building, maintaining and equipping of its schools, for their staffing and finance, and for their efficiency in serving the purposes for which they are intended. It can set up agencies, including sub-committees of the statutory education committee and entrust to these and to managing and governing bodies the performance of some of its functions, but not its responsibility for them. The necessary subordination of the managing or governing body as an *administrative agency* to its parent body are carefully provided for in rules of management and articles of government, but they nevertheless represent a potential challenge, not only to the education committee and the authority, but also to education officers and heads of schools. The Enfield case shows how the skilful evocation of the strictly legal interpretation of articles could delay an authority's implementation of a plan and how clauses relating to the general oversight of the school and of the curriculum overlap with the generally acknowledged responsibility of administrative officers, inspectors and heads.

The interest in school management and government of the Department of Education and Science and its predecessors has been considered at some length. It has three facets:

(1) It is part of the body of assumptions, constituting an administrative mystique, concerning the individuality of the school, the leadership role of the headmaster and the freedom of the teacher. Such assumptions, universally expressed in official publications, are essential for officials working in a situation in which central direction is considered intolerable.

(2) It is part of the carefully worked out series of safeguards, developed over the years, for ensuring that the schools can be

defended against over-hasty education committees and their officers.

(3) Finally, managing and governing bodies are provided for in the Education Act, 1944 and it is the duty of the Department to ensure at least minimum compliance with the intentions of the Act.

On the other hand, teacher associations have had little reason to concern themselves with managing and governing bodies of county schools, although there are many instances in the not too distant past of frequent disputes with the managers of voluntary schools. By and large, the conditions of service and problems of teachers are the concern of administrative officers, heads, inspectors and ultimately the education committee. There is a difference in general attitude between the Joint Four and the N.U.T. and the N.A.S. Especially for heads, the governing body has been a mark of status, which distinguished one secondary school from another; for the N.U.T. and the N.A.S. the managing and governing body has been, if anything, a hindrance, in the direct relations they established with employers.

Now, however, the situation is changing. Teacher associations cannot ignore the need to secure that their members are represented on managing and governing bodies when these are reconstituted to take in parents and members of community groups.

It can, then, be argued that managing and governing bodies operate on the periphery of the network of relationships that constitute the educational system. Moreover, their institutional structure, viewed collectively, is weak. Their members are not held together by common interests, as are salaried officers and teachers; and they are, in the vast majority of cases, the appointees of the education authority. Their position is thus open to invasion by other and more organized interests. Being without anchorage in any structure save that of the local education authorities to which they are subordinate and yet in potential competition, there has been little to keep them from falling completely under its control or the control of political parties associated with it.

THE CONTROL OF MANAGING AND GOVERNING BODIES

It must again be emphasized, despite what has been said, that a managing or governing body is *potentially* a disruptive and un-predictable element. At least theoretically, it is possible to conceive of a governing body which is composed of men and women vigorously opposed to their authority's policy and willing and able to use the law and administrative conventions to prevent it being carried out. Furthermore, one can conceive of a governing body which, whilst not purposely obstructive, would insist in taking a full part in all appointing procedures, and requiring explanations for all changes in curriculum and organization and for fluctuations in examination successes. No instance was found of such a situation existing, but certainly the possibility was present in the minds of heads and others, who cited parent power in American schools, and who were fully alive to the difficulties they might experience from members of organized pressure groups other than the political parties, whose members were willing to follow existing norms.

The most complete form of control is that which is exercised through the control of membership. In extreme cases this means the closing of membership of managing and governing bodies to all save members of the education committee or to councillors; a further step is the provision that the chairman of the education committee and his deputy shall be the chairman and the deputy of a single body dealing with all primary or secondary schools. In less extreme cases the grouping of schools may result in a small number of managing and governing bodies on which committee members and councillors are, in each case, the dominant element. A major argument for grouping is, in fact, that it is only thus that the elected representatives of the community can exercise their responsibilities in the management and government of the schools. In the cases described, of course, control by the education committee or council is synonymous with control by the political party in power. But even where there is no insistence on managing and governing bodies being dominated by elected representatives, places on them are often monopolized by political parties, since they represent a means by which, it is feared, opposing elements could make their voices heard. Moreover, places even on the most inert managing and governing bodies provide political parties with minor means of patronage. Before an election they represent a means by which intending local candidates can add to their store of offices held and thus feel that their claims are made more publicly evident: after an election, they can be used to give some recognition to less prominent party members.

Other and less obvious controls over membership are exercised by managing and governing bodies themselves through their powers to co-opt, where these are exercised; and by the influence that may be exerted by chief education officers and, in some cases, heads. Such influence may not seek to control in the sense of 'inhibit' or 'repress', although this is not infrequently said to be the case. It may be, and often is, exercised to bring forward knowledgeable and useful people holding progressive views in harmony with those of their sponsors. In either case, the result is to bring the managing or governing body concerned within a prevailing or potential orthodoxy shaped by professional leaders.

The effective functioning of managing and governing bodies, however chosen, is very largely dependent upon the chief education officer and his staff and the heads of schools, since it is they who control the channels through which business is brought on to the agenda. Even where issues are raised by managers and governors themselves, as often happens, their treatment depends on the access to information and rulings that only the officers and head can provide. 'Control', in its positive aspects may take the form of the careful selection and presentation of issues to the managers or governors, the attendance of a well-briefed and able clerk, and the supplying of memoranda and reports which direct the attention of the board concerned to relevant issues. In its negative aspects it may take the form of restricting business to formalities by strict monitoring of the agenda and minutes, or by requiring heads' reports to be submitted first through the office. Such practices need not necessarily be considered in a sinister light. Officers and heads operate in a world in which they have to guard the schools against the only too possible errors of judgment or misplaced enthusiasms of their lay colleagues and the timing and presentation of major issues are always a matter of delicate balance.

The control exercised by heads of secondary schools over their governors is generally assumed to be one of the marks of effective headship. Occasions on which heads are challenged are matters of note and suggest that the governors involved have not been 'handled properly'. This means that a head with an active governing body has to know them as individuals and study them as a group; the very process of doing this means that he gauges their possible reactions, and marks out the area within which he can operate in safety. This, in itself, results in a certain limitation of his freedom even if, when he does put an issue to the test, he 'carries his governors with him'. Not what a governing body or committee does or thinks, but what a head or an officer conceives it might do or think can often be decisive.

The chairman, of course, is the key figure, since he must be involved in every item of business submitted to each meeting, and in others that must be dealt with between meetings. But, unless he is a member of the authority or otherwise prominent he may find it difficult to carry weight with the chief education officer and his colleagues. But 'weight' in this sense can be a disadvantage. If, for example, a chairman of governors is also chairman of the education committee or of one of its sub-committees, it is so much the more difficult for him to identify himself with his school if issues of major policy are involved.

In view of the dependence of managing and governing bodies on the support of local authorities, political parties, officers and heads it might be argued that they should cease to have any statutory sanction. The provisions of the Education Act, 1944 and the prescribed machinery of instruments, rules and articles are clearly ineffective in securing to them a place of significance. Should their existence, the form they take and the functions they perform not then be left wholly to the discretion of the local education authorities? This is a point of view which could have been advanced with considerable force some years ago, when the control of social institutions by elected representatives and appointed persons was little challenged. It is, however, more difficult to sustain today.

THE REVIVAL OF OFFICIAL INTEREST

The Royal Commission on Local Government followed the recommendations of the main educational interests in advising that the 'sphere of action open to managers and governors of schools and colleges should be widened.'[3] The Department of Education and Science, in their written evidence, had stated:

In the Department's view, managing and governing bodies of schools are particularly well fitted to express the local community interest in local schools. Their functions are not administrative but consist in part of friendly help and guidance to heads and other teachers and in part in taking certain decisions peculiar to the individual school—about all the appointment when necessary of a new head—which are the close concern of the local community and are within the proper scope of lay people with access to suitable professional advice.

It was further argued that:

. . . any steps which led to each school having its own governing body composed of knowledgeable and enthusiastic people, prepared to take time and trouble over its affairs, would be of great benefit to the schools.[4]

The Association of Education Committees was even more explicit:

. . . we believe it is imperative that there should be a governing body for a school or group of schools, as may be found convenient, and that such governing bodies should have substantial powers.

[3] *Royal Commission on Local Government in England, 1966–69*, Vol. 1 Report, London, H.M.S.O., 1969, para. 318.
[4] Royal Commission on Local Government in England. *Written Evidence of the Department of Education and Science*; London, H.M.S.O., 1967, paras. 108 and 47.

Later, its evidence continues,

They must have freedom to incur expenditure within approved estimates, to appoint teaching and other staff, to determine special allowances and to grant leave of absence in particular cases.[5]

The County Councils Association stated:

Local interest in the service demands the involvement of the community
at a very local level and this can readily be achieved through the
managing or governing bodies of individual schools or groups of schools
and other educational institutions: this form of local management
should be preserved and strengthened whatever pattern of administration by local authorities is adopted for the service.[6]

Much less enthusiastic support for increased significance being
attached to managing and governing bodies came from the
National Association of Divisional Executives and the National
Union of Teachers. The former resisted stoutly the view that, in
the large authorities under consideration, managing and governing
bodies could fill the gap made by the disappearance of divisional
executives, and the National Union of Teachers showed uneasi-
ness at the possibility of managing and governing bodies encroach-
ing on the professional responsibilities of teachers, especially if
they were to exercise to the full their powers of general oversight
of their schools.

In sum, however, though opinions varied as to the part school
managers or governors should or could play within a reformed
structure of local government, their continuance was generally
assumed. They were seen as a necessary counterpoise, at local
level, to the large authorities that it was felt would eventually be
the rule.

---

[5] Association of Education Committees, *Memorandum on Local Government
Re-Organization in England, submitted to the Royal Commission on Local Government
in England,* 1956, paras. 13 and 14.

[6] County Councils Association. *Royal Commission on Local Government in England: Memorandum of Evidence on Proposed Improvements in the Structure of Local
Government and Analysis of existing County Services,* 1966, para. 57.

THE DEMAND FOR PARTICIPATION

This insistence on what, at first sight, appears to be merely the established view restated is supported by moves in the past decade to give greater autonomy and freedom from direct local authority control to colleges of further education and colleges of education. Through the changes which have now taken place following the *Education (No. 2) Act,* 1968, the dominant concept in the government of these institutions is that they are linked with, rather than controlled by, a local education authority or authorities and that through their governing bodies they are in direct relationship with industry and commerce on the one hand and with universities and other educational interests on the other.

There are other trends which contribute to the same end. One is the pressure of the claims increasingly being made by teachers for a share in the government of the schools and colleges in which they work. There are also the claims made by parents, or perhaps more often on their behalf by reformist and radical groups, for them to take some direct share in the conduct and work of the schools.

This trend took early shape in the development of local Associations for the Advancement of State Education, which seek to bring together those interested in the work of the schools and which strive to secure for their members representation on education committees and on managing and governing bodies. It also inspires vigorous and often powerful local campaigns dealing with such issues as secondary school reorganization, policy in relation to school closures, overcrowding and large classes, and the need for more nursery school provision.

There is a third and more general aspect of the movement. This is the increasing dissatisfaction and disregard of representative democracy, especially at the local level, and a turning to 'participation' by all in decisions which concern them.

ATTEMPTS TO REDEFINE THE ROLE OF MANAGERS AND GOVERNORS

By and large the direction of effort is towards developing and refining existing models of school management and government. That is, it is accepted that managing and governing bodies will occupy the same position within the statutory structure as at present, though with increased status. But determined efforts are to be made to define and expand their functions and to broaden their composition.

Thus the Home and School Council, in their booklet, *How to be a School Manager or Governor*,[7] stress the need for managers to visit their schools for the purpose of inspecting the premises and equipment:

Is there proper storage space for bicycles? Is there a safe place for cars and school buses to load and unload? Are there cloakroom facilities for drying wet overcoats and changing wet footwear? Are the premises clean? Are they adequately heated without being stuffy? Are they overcrowded? Is there suitable lighting in classrooms and corridors, and protection from glare in summer? Is there enough storage space and display space? Are there plenty of books in evidence? Are books and equipment well cared for? Are fire precautions adequate and is there a well-established routine for fire drills?

The booklet also advises the regular inspection of school records and accounts, including the punishment book, and gives detailed instructions regarding the interviewing of candidates for appointment.

Another recent booklet, by the Socialist Education Association, *Education Handbook for Labour* (1971), has sections dealing with managers and governors, but has less of the drill manual approach. It warns against visitors setting themselves up as educational experts and also against them being misled by externals. The check-list it provides includes such more general questions as:

[7] Produced by the Home and School Council, at the University of York, 1970.

Are you invited to roam freely and see everything you ask to see, or are you discreetly shepherded?

Do all teachers teach the full range of attainment, or are some (e.g. heads of departments in secondary schools) limited to higher attainment groups?

Does the primary school prepare its children for secondary school with its very different size and organization? Does the secondary school prepare its pupils for life after school?

Such questions, and those already cited from *How to be a School Manager or Governor*, are enough in themselves to show how difficult it is to give positive and detailed guidance to managers and governors, without endowing laymen with quasi-inspectorial powers. Particularly those cited from *Education Handbook for Labour* carry assumptions which are at least questionable.

An approach of a quite different order is presented by the National Association of Governors and Managers in a draft submission for a new Education Act.[8] This sets out five objectives for managing and governing bodies. The first is the 'freedom of head teachers and their staffs to exercise their academic and professional responsibilities in an independent manner'. This is balanced, however, by the second objective which is the 'reflection of the legitimate public interest'. Since schools are public institutions, there is a 'permanent tension between the freedom of the staff and the interest of the public'. This, it is claimed, is a healthy tension, and should also be reflected in managing and governing bodies.

Another objective is that schools and other educational institutions should have a 'measure of self-government', and managing and governing bodies are a means by which teachers and others who work in them can play their part.

As fourth and fifth objective there are the 'fostering of communication and collaboration between parents and staff' and the 'mobilisation of all possible local support behind a particular school'.

From these objectives it is argued that managing and governing

[8] Mimeographed document, 1970.

bodies should include parent and teacher representatives and should also seek to draw in people from varied backgrounds in business, trade union affairs and from other branches of education. It further follows the recommendations made in Research Study 6 of the Royal Commission on Local Government by stressing the need for managers and governors to be easily accessible, in that a list of their names and addresses should be available at the school. Unlike the Research Study, however, it recommends specifically that managing and governing bodies should have more defined powers. Each school should have a budget with heads for staffing, equipment and other purposes. Managers and governors would then have powers of limited *virement*[9] between these heads.

The three publications discussed reveal the difficulties to be encountered in acting upon the very generally expressed view, of which examples have been given, that managing and governing bodies should have a more substantial part to play in the administration of education. The functions which can be assigned to them are those which are already the duties of the administrative officers, inspectors and advisers, acting both as servants of their authority and by the light of their professional knowledge. Moreover, the areas of potential action: the appointment of staff, the inspection of premises, the concern for school-community links are all matters in which heads and teachers are also concerned. For managers and governors to adopt even a marginally more substantial inspectorial and executive role would seem a major reversal of trends, in local government and social administration, towards enlarging the scope for professional decision and action.

It is debateable, then, how far the revitalization and strengthening of managing and governing bodies in the form in which they now exist is what is needed. What may, indeed, be desirable is a structure for administrative action on a day-to-day basis, backed by statutory powers and set within the framework of representative democracy, but rather a structure for the focussing of local opinion. As Self has argued, 'genuinely small-scale government has

[9] The technical term for internal reallocation of expenditure within an already approved global figure.

ceased, save in an advisory capacity, to be a practical possibility'.[10] It is the search for such a structure that has given rise to the new concepts of democratic involvement expounded in different ways in the Skeffington and Redcliffe-Maud reports and which has been given theoretical formulation in a recent study by Carole Pateman, to which reference will be made later.

THE SKEFFINGTON REPORT

The Skeffington report on *People and Planning* is specifically concerned with town and country planning, but in so doing it concerns itself with the total context of political action at local level.

It may be that the evolution of the structures of representative government which has concerned western nations for the last century and a half is now entering into a new phase. There is a growing demand by many groups for more opportunity to contribute and for more say in the working out of policies which affect people not merely at election time, but continuously as proposals are being hammered out and, certainly, as they are being implemented. Life, so the argument runs, is becoming more and more complex, and one cannot leave all the problems to one's representatives. They need some help in reaching the right decision, and opportunity should be provided for discussions with all those involved.[11]

Certainly, provision for the citizen to take part in local government has hitherto been largely a matter of work in political parties or, in a minority of cases, in committees and sub-committees concerned with the minutiae of routine administration. The Skeffington report opens the way for a more widely diffused form of participation. It envisages people being more widely informed of what future action is being planned, of their being encouraged to participate in surveys and other activities, and of their being helped by information expertly provided. There is an imaginative

[10] Self, Peter, *Bureaucracy or Management. An Inaugural Lecture*, L.S.E., 1965.

[11] Ministry of Housing and Local Government. Report of the (Skeffington) Committee on Public Participation in Planning, People and Planning, H.M.S.O., 1969, p. 11.

suggestion that community forums should be set up. These would 'provide local organizations with the opportunity to discuss collectively planning and other issues of importance and also have administrative functions such as receiving and distributing information on planning matters and promoting the formation of neighbourhood groups'. Within such a setting managing and governing bodies would have an important part to play, by contributing through their members to local forums and neighbourhood groups by sharing in the information services to which they, in turn, would contribute.

THE REDCLIFFE-MAUD PROPOSALS

The Skeffington report was concerned with setting up a wide and varied series of means by which participation in town and country planning can be secured. The Royal Commission on Local Government was also concerned in developing means for ensuring more effective popular participation and it too emphasized that these must be mainly advisory in character. It advanced, in particular, the idea of the *local council*, to take the place of all borough, urban district and rural district councils and parish councils. These councils were not to overlap in functions with statutory authorities:

We do not see them as having statutory responsibility for any local government service; but we do see them as contributing a vital element to democratic local government. Their key function should be to focus opinion about anything that affects the well-being of each community, and to bring it to bear on the responsible authorities; but in addition they should have a number of powers to be exercised at discretion.[12]

Later, the report states:

The most important function of the local councils, common to all from the smallest to the biggest, will be the duty to voice the opinions and wishes of the local community . . . the main authority should be

---

[12] Royal Commission on Local Government in England, 1966–1969 (Chairman: The Rt. Hon. Lord Redcliffe-Maud), Cmnd. 4040, H.M.S.O., 1969, para. 371.

obliged to consult a local council before taking any decision which would particularly affect its area, and to give a local council the opportunity to comment on proposed development of any significance; and local officials of the main authority should keep as closely in touch with local councils as practicable. But local councils should not act only when consulted. It will be their responsibility to see that the views and wishes of their inhabitants about any local government service, or any other matter of concern to the local community, are made known to the responsible authorities.[13]

In many respects the role of managing and governing bodies can be viewed as similar to that of the local council. Like the latter they cannot have final responsibility for the schools or any other aspect of the local education service, although they do and should continue to form part of the statutory structure. As in the case of the local council, also, the main authority should be obliged to consult managers and governors before taking any decision that would particularly affect their school, and also to give managers and governors the opportunity to comment on proposed developments of any significance. Clearly, too, managers and governors should not act only when consulted. It should be their responsibility also to see that the views and wishes of all those concerned in the affairs of their school should be made known to the responsible authorities. Such a conception obviates the need to find a niche for managing and governing bodies within the executive process. They will not be left to justify their existence by the extent to which they can wrest the making of routine decisions from administrators and teachers, but they will form part of a powerful structure for formulating and giving expression to public opinion.

There is no reason, also, why managing and governing bodies should not, in this setting, develop financial resources of their own. They could, also, be a means by which LEAs anxious to provide a park or children's playground, could arouse interest amongst those most likely to further such a project.

13 ibid., para. 381.

REPRESENTATION OR PARTICIPATION

The proposals of the Skeffington and the Redcliffe-Maud reports which have just been discussed seek to supplement the existing machinery of local government by agencies, whether community forums or local councils, which make it possible for far more people to participate in opinion-forming as distinct from merely voting.

The issues which this raises are discussed at length in *Participation and Democratic Theory*,[14] by Carole Pateman who draws a distinction between what she terms classical democracy and participatory democracy. In the former the emphasis is on government through representatives. The role of the ordinary man is to elect those who will make decisions on his behalf; it is 'competition between leaders for votes that is the characteristically democratic element in this political method'. 'Participation', so far as the majority is concerned is, according to Pateman, 'participation in the choice of decision-makers'. Once elected, representatives are responsible for the conduct of affairs and further 'participation' is seen as an encroachment on their authority. The practices of those authorities which give minimum support to the principles of school management and government can be interpreted in the light of this theory. Either managing and governing bodies must consist of those who are elected and who are therefore 'responsible', and/or they must be deprived of any real participation in decision-making.

Against this approach Carole Pateman erects a theory of 'participatory democracy', built up from the teachings of Rousseau, J. S. Mill and G. D. H. Cole. This theory is 'built round the central assertion that individuals and their institutions cannot be considered in isolation from one another.' Interaction between people and institutions must take place at all levels, and cannot be reduced to interaction through representatives. In this way people are educated to participate *through* participation. Individual, institution and society are seen, not as discrete and separate

[14] Oxford University Press, 1970.

entities, but each as being one aspect of a network of relationships. Within this concept of participatory democracy, the community council, the local council and the neighbourhood council clearly have their theoretical underpinnings.

Further light is thrown on the two aspects of democracy, but from a different point of view, by Richard Wollheim.[15] He points out that

. . . we need to take account of an ambiguity, or perhaps a duality, in the nature of representative assemblies. For, on the one hand, we may see such assemblies as primarily the places where action, action of a social or political kind, is taken. Representative assemblies so understood help to satisfy the definition of a democracy as a form of government where ultimately (i.e., *via* the representatives) power rests with the people. On the other hand, we may also see representative assemblies as primarily the places where discussion or debate occurs: discussion or debate, on the whole, about what social or political action, if any, is to be taken. Such a view of representative assemblies corresponds, of course, to the idea or conception of government as essentially government by discussion. We may call the first view the 'legislative' conception of the democratic assembly, and the second view the 'deliberative' conception.

Whilst Wollheim is thinking in terms of national political institutions, the distinction which he draws between the legislative and deliberative functions holds good equally well in the context of local government or indeed any form of committee-controlled activity. He argues, for example, that

The legislative conception demands that the policy that enjoys a majority in the country should have a working majority amongst the representatives: which may well mean that the ratio of supporters to opponents in the country should be exaggerated in the assembly. On the other hand, the deliberative conception demands that every significant shade of opinion be represented, and to achieve this it might even be necessary to increase the representation of minorities beyond the proportionate size.

[15] In a joint paper with A. Phillips Griffiths, 'How can one person represent another?' in *Proc. Arist. Soc.*, Supplementary Volume XXXIV (1960), pp. 209–24.

Clearly, the demand that managing and governing bodies should reflect the political complexion of their parent local authority corresponds to the 'legislative conception'; and the demand that managing and governing bodies should represent teacher, parent, and community interests reflects the 'deliberative conception'.

Similar conclusions are reached by W. Hampton, in his study of Sheffield politics.[16] He argues that orthodox elected councils cannot be expected to devise and control policy effectively and at the same time involve people in general in local community affairs. There is a consequent need for a network of single-purpose community organizations, not sharing in the executive functions of local government, but rather performing a monitoring and supportive role.[17]

[16] *Democracy and Community*, Oxford University Press, 1970.
[17] Since the research on which this book is based was completed, there has been a number of reports of changes instituted by local authorities in their systems of school management and government. Most appear to have taken the form of providing or increasing provision for teachers and parents to serve as managers and governors, and for giving each school its own managing or governing body. In the Inner London Education Authority, this is now the accepted pattern. But care has been taken, by increasing the size of both managing and governing bodies, to ensure that a majority of those serving are nominees of the authority. There has been no change in the nature of the relationship which has existed between the managing and governing bodies and the authority on the one hand and the community on the other.

Most other authorities which have instituted changes have followed the same policy of widening membership (even in one or two cases, to appointing senior pupils as governors) without changing the balance of interests in their managing and governing bodies. The most distinctively new pattern appears to have developed in Sheffield (interestingly enough, in view of Hampton's *Democracy and Community*). Here there were until 1970, no managing bodies for primary schools or governing bodies for groups of schools. But the present pattern provides for a managing body for each primary school and for each secondary school: and these include not only headteachers and representatives of teachers in the schools but also parents and non-teaching staff. An innovation of particular interest is that of cross-representation: that is, managing bodies include a member of the local secondary school governing body, whilst the governing bodies recruit one of their number from among the managers of a contributory primary school. Finally, the managers and governors co-opt two others. There is no pressure on them to choose councillors or others with political party affiliations; if councillors do serve, they have no prescriptive right to chairmanships.

A NEW STRUCTURE FOR SCHOOL
MANAGEMENT AND GOVERNMENT

The significance of this kind of thinking for school management and government is obvious. It at least suggests that it is no longer necessary to look upon managing and governing bodies as being minor elements in the same structure as local education authorities. They can be seen, in part at least, as important elements in the new structure of popular participation that the Skeffington and Redcliffe-Maud reports have so strikingly outlined.

First, with regard to the school itself:

(1) They should receive, debate and act on reports and information relating to the organization and curriculum of their schools.

(2) They should be given full information on financial estimates and matters relating to buildings and equipment and their recommendations in these matters should carry real weight with the education committee and its sub-committees.

(3) They should be felt, both by head and staff, to be able to enter sympathetically into public debate regarding controversies in which the school is involved.

(4) They should, as now, play a leading role in the appointment of heads of schools and should, especially through their chairman, act with heads in matters of discipline in which community interest is involved and community support is essential.

At present managers and governors have very little direct access to public opinion, save through the local education authority and the channels it provides. The local forums and neighbourhood groups of the Skeffington report could provide managers and governors with an important role, both in giving and receiving information and comment. They would be strategically placed to be a leaven in discussions on planning in relation to education and in help in the development of informed public opinion.

Can changes of this kind, however, ensure that managers and governors will have the degree of independence that will enable them to function effectively, without at the same time diminishing the essential powers of local education authorities? A solution might be that managing and governing bodies should not only be linked administratively with their 'parent' local education authority, but also that some measure of co-ordination should be achieved by the setting up of a new national agency composed of nominees of the Department of Education and Science and the Department of the Environment, of local education authorities, of teacher associations and of interest groups of parents and others. This agency would not only recommend approval of formal Instruments, Rules and Articles, but also advise and comment on their application in specific instances. It would also collect and disseminate information about current practices and issues and, through its reports, provide a background of knowledge and discussion that is so clearly lacking at the present time. The activities of this agency might well form one aspect of the work of the Local Government Central Office such as that recommended in the *Committee on Management of Local Government* (1967). This agency, it will be recalled, was to be concerned with reviewing the powers of local authorities, with carrying out or promoting research and with providing a source of information and advice to members.

Such an approach might meet the often expressed concern that the constitutions of governing and managing bodies should allow a wide range of lay and professional interests an opportunity of contributing to the welfare of the schools, while preserving a direct link with the political control of the areas they serve.

As the research project showed, parents serve on about half of all governing bodies as individuals. The difficulty in arranging for more systematic participation lies in defining the 'constituency' to be represented. There is still some resistance, especially by heads of primary schools, to giving rights of representation to parent associations, which may reflect the interests of a minority of able organizers, or fall under the control of extreme groups. There are also organizational difficulties, though they need not prove insuperable, as the Inner London Education Authority has demonstrated, in parent representatives being elected from the total parent 'population' associated with a school.

The resistance to teachers serving on managing and governing bodies at the time when the research surveys were being made was considerable. It was based on the general objection felt to public servants controlling their own conditions of employment, and to the objection raised by those who feel that people working together should not determine each other's promotion prospects. Now, however, a number of authorities have made provision for teacher representation.

It is questionable how far the present concept of a managing and governing body can, and should be expected to balance interest groups. Either such interests, invariably themselves diverse, have to be limited to one or two representatives, or they have to become unduly large. It would seem, then, that experiments might be made with managers/governors-parents and managers/governors-staff sub-committees, which would consider selected issues of common concern and make what representations might appear desirable to the full governing body. In this way more parents and more teachers could be involved in the advisory functions of managing and governing bodies than would be possible if two or three places only were reserved for each category on managing and governing bodies themselves.

There is a further suggestion which might be considered and which might prove more valuable than at first sight may appear likely. It is that a number of places on managing and governing bodies, and more especially on the sub-committees just referred to, should be filled by partial self-selection.

Election as a method of filling places on councils, committees and boards depends upon certain assumptions: that electors and elected have common and known interests, and that the electors can identify those candidates whom they feel will serve them best. Such conditions only exist where effective machinery for participation has been introduced and accepted through political or other interest groups or where, as in a social or sports club, individuals are known to each other. Where they do not exist there are two possibilities:

either, elections to minor bodies fall under the control of political parties or groups and other organizations with little direct concern in the institutions involved. Often, indeed, the representatives sent forward are the only ones available.

or, elections are held, as at parents meetings, where nominations are received and voting takes place in an assembly in which most present are unknown to each other. Those who might wish to serve and who have a contribution to make are often overlooked.

It has been seen that some authorities have tried to widen their field of recruitment of managers and governors by advertising for candidates. In this way it was hoped to secure interested people who would otherwise not be found. This idea might be extended. The Skeffington Report recommends that planning authorities should consider setting up Participants' Registers in which the names of people and bodies could be entered, who wish to be kept informed of the preparation of development plans. It should not be impossible to devise a register on somewhat similar lines for prospective managers and governors. A pool would thus be created from which cooptative governors could be drawn.

Such a system would certainly help in respect of those who were neither members of political parties, parents or teachers, or locally well-known. It could contribute in securing members drawn from a wide spread of social class, religious and (in an increasing number of areas) racial backgrounds. An element of self-selection from those who might otherwise remain out of reach might help, at least initially, in arousing interest and also in providing a body of persons for whom conferences and courses for prospective managers and governors might be organized.

More than most of our institutions the managing and governing bodies of our schools show the inadequacy, in the urban, technological and impersonal society in which we live, of earlier political and administrative models, with their over-emphasis on the decision-making as opposed to the decision-influencing agencies. with their narrow view of accountability, and with their assumption that participation of all kinds must be thought of in terms of the representation of major political and other interest groups. Because of their dependent position managing and governing bodies display, often in an acute form, the atrophying influence of such models. Their reform may point the way to means by which constructive modes of participation may be developed in many kinds of institutions and services.

Appendix 1: Theory and Research in Local Government

D. A. HOWELL

The current state of local government studies in England has naturally conditioned our own approach. In particular this has been limited by the lack of a developed theoretical base, and by a shortage of large scale field studies. There has indeed been little cause to modify what one of us wrote in 1969 in describing the principal objectives which should be pursued in the study of educational administration (G. Baron and W. Taylor (eds), *Educational Administration and the Social Sciences*, pp. 13–14):

There are two major tasks that lie ahead, although beginnings have been made in respect of both. The first is that of making known and demonstrating the relevance of concepts and approaches that already exist within the social sciences and that have a bearing on the study of educational policy and administration. Role theory from sociology, the concept of cost-benefit analysis from economics, pressure group theory from political science, group dynamics from psychology, all have their special contribution to make. From these concepts and others related to them there may be built up an approach to the study of educational administration that gives it the theoretical bases of which it is so much in need.

The second task is, against the background just indicated, to construct through investigation and research, a body of case studies from which systematic content can be developed.

With regard to the more theoretical task, most general theories of organization are not in a position to give a satisfactory account of highly complex systems, to judge by W. J. M. Mackenzie's claim in *Politics and Social Science* (1967), p. 352, that so far general systems theory has had little or nothing to contribute to the study of local or regional political systems, among which LEAs must surely be included. The lack of a developed theoretical base led Mackenzie on another occasion (in his Greater London Paper 'Theories of local government', L.S.E., 1961) to claim that there was indeed no theory of local government and to ask whether anything significant had happened since John Stuart Mill. And, moreover, educational administration is one aspect of local government which has received conspicuously less attention from academics than its intrinsic importance warrants. In these circumstances the research worker can contribute only to less general theories or hypotheses, and in this context it is suggested that the present study may be of some interest for the light which it throws on the concept of representative government and its application to educational administration, and on the interaction of laymen and professional officers within a democratic system. If it is out of the question to develop a general theory, then by exploring the field without necessarily testing any major hypothesis one can at least say something about the principles or assumptions which are commonly invoked or challenged by those engaged in the field.

(When the above was already in the press, two books were published which indicate a very substantial advance in the theoretical study of local government: M. J. Hill, *The Sociology of Public Administration* (1972), and P. Self, *Administrative Theories and Politics* (1972)).

For this purpose one needs to perform the second of the two tasks indicated above, namely develop a body of case studies. It is in this context that we wish to stress the importance of own research, since it represents almost the first sustained attempt to study the workings of educational administration, even though this is by far the largest local government commitment at present. It is true that secondary school re-organization has prompted some limited area studies, like that of R. Batley, O. R. O'Brien, and H. Parris on Darlington and Gateshead,[1] but until recently little has been learnt about the operations of local authorities from studies of individual localities. Studies like those by H. V. Wiseman of

[1] *Going Comprehensive*, Routledge and Kegan Paul, 1970.

Leeds,[2] F. Bealey and J. Blondel of Newcastle-under-Lyme,[3] G. W. Jones of Wolverhampton,[4] and most recently W. Hampton of Sheffield[5] have been concerned primarily with the workings of local political parties or pressure groups and not with the operation of the services which they control. Our concern with concrete matters is therefore inherent both in the nature of the subject and the state of research into local government.

The methodological foundations for studies like ours were laid in Donnison and Chapman's *Social Policy and Administration* (1965), in which the development of social services at the local level was studied through the medium of analysing particular decisions. Again, in education at least, this approach has not really been developed. A particular feature of our own research is that although it deals with a multiplicity of minor administrative agencies, it is concerned also with the detailed examination of a a single aspect of educational administration as it has been developed and modified over the past century in England.

METHODS AND RESEARCH

Studies of political institutions and administrative processes can be carried out through the scrutiny of documentary evidence, through interviews and questionnaires, and by direct observation. Each approach has its own particular limitations, and each may be more appropriate at a different level of enquiry, but collectively they can provide a reasonably full and convincing picture.

Documentary evidence, and in particular articles and instruments of government indicate the legal framework within which governing bodies operate, and which sets limits to their activities. While they are essential in that they indicate official intentions and policies they are incomplete in that they say nothing about the full range of possible activities or relationships of the parties involved,

[2] *Local Government at Work*, Routledge and Kegan Paul, 1967.
[3] *Constituency Politics*, Faber and Faber, 1965.
[4] *Borough Politics*, Oxford University Press, 1969.
[5] *Democracy and Community*, Oxford University Press, 1970.

or about the subtleties of influence as opposed to the distribution of formal powers. Moreover they are frequently out of date and seldom followed to the letter. They do not furnish any information about the political or other factors determining the selection of governors, while the articles of government are not to be relied on to reveal what the governors actually do. They serve, however, to limit the area of possible action and to provide guide lines for investigation and research.

Records and correspondence make it possible to undertake illuminating case studies especially where the issues under consideration relate mainly to negotiations between bodies with independent decision-making powers, where one can trace successive steps and identify crucial developments. Some outstanding examples of studies of parallel significance are those described in the successive volumes of F. M. G. Willson's *Administrators in Action* (various dates) even though as the author admits (p. 30 of the 1961 edition) there are considerable limitations in that the account of (e.g.) Coventry's acquisition of its new market is one-sided, being based on the Corporation's records only.

Questionnaires and interviews can be regarded as complementary research tools. Questionnaires provide an economical method of gathering information on matters of opinion and attitude as well as fact from substantial numbers of people, who may be widely scattered and whom it is out of the question to interview individually. Difficulties centre round the achievement of an adequate response rate, the ambiguity or inadequacy of written answers, and a certain reluctance among respondents to reply to lengthy questionnaires or to give other than stock answers. Moreover there are special problems involved in the issue of questionnaires when studying systems of school government as opposed to individual governing bodies. A questionnaire sent to a head or governor and asking for information about the operations of his own governing body will get reasonably specific answers, because the questions themselves are interpreted with reference to one body only; when dealing with a system as a whole, a questionnaire may well produce only the most general and superficial answers in such terms as 'it depends', 'from time to time', and so forth. Moreover, the completion of the questionnaire may be treated as a routine exercise and be handed over to a comparatively junior officer. Alternatively the answers may reflect a blurred consensus of the views of senior officers concerned with school government.

When it is a matter of finding out what happens in a large local education authority, in which practice may vary as from division to division and from school to school, either one has to be satisfied with general answers to general questions or one has to have fore-knowledge of all the possible variations of practice that may be found. Even if the latter are already known, to deal with them adequately demands a questionnaire of unmanageable complexity.

Interviewing is therefore necessary if one is to obtain reliable and exact information and authoritative views from those persons or interests principally involved in school government. In particular, semi-structured interviews make it easier to follow up promising leads, or to press when vague or general or stock answers are given. If the interviewer deals with several participants, each of whom gives his own account of how the system works, he will then be in a position to ask respondent B for his comments on respondent A's account of any one incident. Such series of interviews have their uses not simply in checking the accuracy of what individuals have said, nor in revealing biased or partisan views, but also in bringing to light different conceptions about the purpose and functioning of the local system. Although recollections may be distorted, interviews can be extremely informative and more revealing than records or questionnaires, particularly on matters concerning attitudes, influence, effectiveness and personal relationships. As a guide to the structuring of information gained from interviews, the model developed by Donnison and Chapman (op. cit., Chapter 3) for the analysis of administration could, we found, be used with some advantage. This model distinguishes (1) the official or authorized version written into the constitution of an agency (2) the interpretation given by people working in the agency, explaining how the official version has in practice been developed and modified (3) the observer's own conclusions designed to approximate as closely as possible to 'administration as it really is' (4) the observer's opinions about the tasks organizations and procedures which are advocated as those which the agency ought to develop for the future. On this basis we distinguish between the official version as laid down by the instruments and articles of government, and the participant's own interpretations of the system as it has been developed and modified. Whether the reconciliation of conflicting interpretations enables us to provide an adequate account of the way the system 'really' works may be open to question; possibly such a state of objectivity cannot be attained, but even so one can detect how far participants are aware of each other's interest and outlooks and then proceed to Donnison's final stage and, as we attempted in Chapter 8, to form opinions about the tasks, organizations and procedures which need to be adopted.

To study individual governing bodies in action, it is necessary to collect information from members of identifiable and accessible participant groups. Coverage of this order gives material comparable to that obtained from the CEOs and the groups or interest principally involved can be identified as heads, governors, administration officers, and parents. It is easy to send questionnaires to representative samples of major groups which are organized on a national basis or which are accessible through LEAs, and by this means samples of heads, governors and administrative officers were included.

For a more detailed examination of school government a series of case studies was planned to take account of widely different social and administrative conditions within LEAs. The authorities selected included two large counties completely organized on a divisional basis, two medium sized counties with both divisional executives and local administrative offices, and one smallish county with locally resident clerks. The county boroughs comprised three large ones where secondary reorganization was well advanced, and where the system of school government had been recast with the object of giving governors more scope, and one medium and two small county boroughs which had governing bodies for each school or pair of adjacent schools. In addition a separate study was made of the unique system found in the Inner London Education Authority. During the course of these case studies occasional use was made of observation as well as interviews, as the staff of the research unit were able to attend governors meetings.

The scope of direct observation within our research was limited to giving the research staff an opportunity of seeing governing bodies at work. As a technique however, it could have been developed only with a massive increase in resources: even so it is doubtful how much more illumination would have been gained through sitting in at one or two meetings, and it would also have been necessary to interview participants subsequently to obtain their explanation of what went on and why. Clearly observation could contribute much more in a linear study of school government in one or two authorities over a lengthy period, but it was inappropriate to a national study carried out over a shorter time.

THE COLLECTION OF DATA

The data for the research was collected by the following means:

(1) By the study of Governmental publications and of debates in Hansard.

(2) Through collection of copies of instruments and articles of government and other documents produced by LEAs.

(3) By examination of file material at the Public Records Office and elsewhere.

(4) Through interviews with Chief Education Officers or their representatives in every local education authority in England.

(5) By sample surveys among the membership of those organizations principally concerned.

(6) By detailed studies of individual local education authorities.

A fuller account must now be given of each source of information.

THE STUDY OF GOVERNMENT PUBLICATIONS AND HANSARD

The preparation of the 1944 Act and its passage through Parliament and the execution of the new statutory requirements by LEAs are the principal occasions on which our main sources were provided by Government publications and Hansard reports. The publications consisted of:

(a) The White Paper *Educational Reconstruction* (Cmd. 6458/1943).

(b) The text of the Education Bill and of the subsequent (1944) Act, in its provisions relation to governing bodies.

(c) The Command Paper *Principles of Government in Maintained Secondary Schools* (Cmd. 6523/1944).

(d) The Model Articles issued by the Ministry.

The terms of the Bill and the Act represent the final result only of governmental thinking, as no record was available of the Board's consultations with representative organizations or interested parties. The passage of the Bill through Parliament is recorded in Hansard, which indicates the level of political interest in school government and the extent to which the government accepted or resisted pressures for change. Subsequently and especially after the issue of the Command Paper, the place of governing bodies in the educational system was considered to be established. It was not evidently thought necessary to issue any further general guidance but to solve particular problems as they were presented by individual LEAs.

The question of parental representation on governing bodies illustrates how far LEAs thought themselves free to go their own way and disregard official and political encouragement. This principle had been commended in Parliamentary debate, accepted as sound by the President of the Board and encouraged in the Command Paper. However, no steps were taken to transform this general encouragement into a specific national policy requirement, or even to examine why so many LEAs were reluctant to provide for parents on governing bodies. In other words it is clear that the terms of Ministerial pronouncement, on even specific provisions, provide no guarantee of local compliance.

INSTRUMENTS AND ARTICLES OF GOVERNMENT

Copies of these documents were obtained from every local education authority, and the range of provision and the chief variations were listed and classified. Major departures from the common form produced in the Model Articles issued by the Ministry of Education after the 1944 Act were noted.

Some shortcomings in the utility of these documents will be apparent from earlier sections of this book. In particular, some instruments of government give no indication of the number of schools to be served by each governing body or of the difficulties met in filling each of the prescribed categories of governor. As a guide to the activities of governing bodies, the articles are by no means complete. They do not by any means cover all aspects of governors' work and they frequently lag behind current practice. Moreover identical provisions can be interpreted and applied in very different ways. Although the consent of the DES is needed for variation of formal provisions, it is clear the LEAs are more likely to change their practice without seeking consent every time.

The basic incompleteness of the provisions of articles of government derives mainly from the limited guidance given by the Ministry after 1944. In particular there is little construction put by the Ministry on the interpretation of key passages such as those relating to 'governors' oversight of the school and its curriculum'. The close resemblance of the model articles to those issued in 1908 for the then newly established County Secondary Schools has already been noted, and this indicates that there was little fresh thinking about the place of governing bodies when the 1944 Bill was being prepared. In these circumstances it was possible for LEAs to include provisions in their articles which emphasized out of date, obsolete or meaningless functions. Sometimes—quite recently too—the governors' concerns have been spelt out in extraordinary detail, as for example in the Outer London Borough where the Articles issued in 1965, empower the governors 'to make reasonable regulations regarding pupils' dress and uniform, with particular reference to the length of hair and wearing of jewellery.'

FILE MATERIAL RELATING TO LEAS

For the inter-war period, correspondence between LEAs or governing bodies and the Board of Education, and other documentary material relating to governing bodies was examined. The availability of this material ensures that the part played by each of the three major parties could be studies at first hand, although it should be made clear that the material deals essentially only with issues which LEAs and governing bodies were not able to resolve satisfactorily on their own, or where it was necessary for the Board of Education to give decision or consent. This material therefore does not give a complete picture about initiative at local level, or indeed about local repercussions after the Board's decisions. And sometimes weeding of material has left gaps. Nevertheless sufficient episodes can be traced to convey the general character of the Board of Education and LEA relationships during this period, as far as governing bodies are concerned. They consist of little more than a series of spasmodic local difficulties which nevertheless could and did smoulder on for a long time unless well handled. The material does give a better idea of the Board of Education's interest in governing bodies, than of the activities of governing bodies themselves or of LEA interest in them, except for the pioneering ideas of Henry Morris shortly after the Hadow report.

Post-war material from the Ministry (subsequently the Department) was used in connection with the information given in the course of interviews with Chief Education Officers. The material was sufficient to describe a small number of cases in the field of central local relations. The chapter dealing with central/local relations may be seen as a pendant to J. A. G. Griffith's classic study,[6] and in particular to his observations (p. 559f.) about deficiencies in the information gathering services of government departments. The Department was asked to amplify the accounts already given by CEOs (and confirmed by the LEAs own files) and a summary of records and minutes with a bearing on the issues at stake was produced. This made it apparent that particular stress was laid on the need to get the views of HMIs as well as officers of the administrative branch concerned. Study of this material, and discussion with DES officers made it clear that it was more common for DES to give informal advice than to insist on securing statutory approval for all minor modifications in current schemes of government, and this must be commended as sound administrative practice. However, it must be said that at times some officers in DES were apparently concerned more with the formalities of the constitution than with the realities of life in schools and education offices. There was virtually no check by DES on the extent to which LEAs were complying with national policy. They were left alone except when proposed changes in the formal provisions were brought to the Department's notice. Great importance was attached to the HMI's knowledge of individual LEAs and CEOs, and it seems clear that many of the officers concerned with this aspect of education did not really know what was going on in the localities.

(1) *The Chief Education Officers*

All CEOs in England were asked if they would be willing to discuss school government with a member of the research unit. In the introductory letter a full explanation was given of the scope of the research, the auspices under which it was being carried out, and the results it was hoped to obtain. CEOs were also asked to send copies of instruments and articles of government, together with any other papers considered relevant. Only one CEO out of 166 refused to participate, on the grounds that as his authority had no separate governing bodies there would be no point in a visit, but even he sent a copy of the articles and instruments. This degree of

[6] *Central Departments and Local Authorities*, Allen & Unwin, 1966.

cooperation must be regarded as quite outstanding; several CEOs mentioned the increasing demands on their time being made by research workers, and some hinted that they were flattering the unit by making an exception to their usual policy of refusing requests for assistance. Many CEOs had obviously taken a great deal of trouble to prepare for their interview and they were also ready to provide further details subsequently. The interview schedule, which was piloted with half a dozen CEOs, was designed to cover every general aspect of school government, and was not administered in a completely uniform fashion. People of the standing of CEOs expect to have the opportunity of talking about professional activities in their own way, and it was tactically undesirable to insist that all interviews should follow the same pattern throughout. Paramount importance was attached to getting the CEOs to talk freely, and the research requirements were met as long as the interviewers were able to cover all matters included in the interview schedule. After each interview notes, often running to a dozen pages or so, were written up and later a digest was prepared as a basis for analysis.

Interviews varied in length and scope. At one extreme, there was a bare half hour of one sentence answers, at the other almost a full day was spent going round the education department talking to a succession of administrative and professional officers. Elsewhere interviewers were confronted with a brains trust of officers who revealed considerable divergences of outlook. As interviewers gained the confidence of the CEOs the latter warmed to their subject, and talked a great deal about current matters, including confidential and indeed explosive problems which would certainly not have been mentioned in any written answers. Some CEOs volunteered information about practices in neighbouring authorities; others were intrigued or astonished to learn attitudes or practices encountered elsewhere. At times, and particularly in small country boroughs, interviewers were surprised at the isolation and lack of awareness shown of developments even in neighbouring authorities. The initial letter to CEOs had stressed that all information given would be treated as strictly confidential, and that no reference would be made to any single authority or school. As a result of this undertaking, much valuable information supported by detailed documentation was often given.

(2) *The sample enquiries*

As indicated earlier, four main groups or interests were identified as concerned with school government, namely heads, governors themselves, administrative officers and parent groups. Naturally, the organizational structure of these interests determined the method of approach, and for all groups except the parents there were no difficulties in securing satisfactory coverage. The heads were the easiest group to approach systematically and two sample enquiries were carried out. The first was from the ranks of the Headmasters Association and the Association of Headmistresses, whose members were at the time highly concentrated in selective secondary schools. Fruitful discussions were held with representatives of the National Union of Teachers and the National Association of Head Teachers; the Executive Committee of the latter were kind enough to make available the results of a survey conducted among their own membership, but the records of neither body were organized on a basis which would permit drawing a sample of their members without undue pressure on the unit's or the associations' own staffing and financial resources.

For all the sample enquiries, a procedure was adopted of using open-ended questions covering the same general topics as the interview schedule, but adapted where necessary to allow the respondents to write about their own specific attitudes and interests. The HMA/AHM questionnaire was discussed with representatives of the two organizations who agreed to give the enquiry official support and thereby undoubtedly enhanced the response rate. This questionnaire was sent to a 1 in 5 national sample of heads in membership of these two associations, drawn from current membership lists, and excluding those in independent or Roman Catholic aided schools. The final response, after three reminders, was over 82 per cent (289 out of 352) which is very satisfactory in view of the comments made by many heads about the timing, length and complexity of the questionnaire. To counteract the bias inherent in this enquiry a random sample of county secondary schools heads was drawn from the lists in the current Education Committees Year Book, and the same questionnaire was sent later to a 1 in 10 sample; on the rare occasions when this sampling presented us with a school already chosen the previous school in the list was taken. The overall response to this questionnaire was slightly lower, being nearly 79 per cent (436 out of 553).

There was a means of direct access to an important group of school governors. Virtually all English Universities nominated representatives to serve on governing bodies of (in the main) selective secondary schools. Not every LEA had provision for University representation on governing bodies, some for policy reasons, others because there was no University within range; and some universities were asked to supply large numbers of governors, not necessarily university teachers, but possibly members of Convocation or the Guild of Graduates, or simply graduates resident in the area. Every registrar of an English University was approached, and all supplied a list of governors and of the schools to which they were attached. Some Registrars wrote in detail to explain the principles on which appointments were made, thus enabling the unit to again identify different groups within this sample, e.g. teaching staff from Departments and Institutes of Education, other university teachers, administrative and other staff, members of Convocation or its equivalent, and locally resident graduates. The questionnaire was sent to a 1 in 2 sample of governors of aided and maintained schools and produced a response rate of 83 per cent (308 out of 371). It was similar to that sent to Heads but some of the questions were framed with the interests of the University governors in mind.

The third nationally accessible source consists of the Divisional Education Officers in Divisional Executives and Excepted Districts. Their views supplement those of the CEOs. Almost invariably one of the functions of a Divisional Officer is to act as clerk to the governing bodies, and for these reasons they could be expected to be very much aware of relationships between governors, heads and the local community. They would also be able to give a great deal of information about the operation of different schemes of divisional administration in so far as they bore on school government. The questionnaire sent to all DEOs in England secured a response rate of 82 per cent (131 out of 159). A considerable amount of factual material pertaining to the operation of divisional executive and their relationships to governing bodies was collected, and DEOs were also asked to give their comments on the respective functions of divisional executives and governing bodies within the same administrative system.

It was unfortunately not possible to undertake a systematic survey of the role of parents on governing bodies, through parent teacher associations or Associations for the Advancement of State Education: the coverage of these bodies is patchy, and it seemed more realistic to include consideration of the case for parental governors as part of the plans for detailed local case studies.

(3) *The case studies*

As mentioned earlier these were based on Local Education Authorities and not on individual schools. It was quite clearly out of the question to consider the school in isolation from the LEA. In essentials the case studies followed a common pattern, although a completely stereotyped approach was wholly inappropriate, as systems of school government vary so greatly, and it was necessary to work out the most effective method of study for each authority separately. In one fairly small county borough all secondary schools were included; elsewhere a proportion had to be selected and the basis of selection varied from authority to authority. It was essential to obtain a good spread of schools of all sizes, ages and categories, and serving different kinds of area; for this purpose local knowledge was necessary, while a completely random selection by the unit might not have produced sharply contrasting schools. The schools were therefore chosen by the unit in consultation with the CEO, but this method has not, as far as we know, produced a distorted or in particular an idealized picture of school government. There might possibly have been a tendency for CEOs to suggest schools whose heads would offer the most glowing picture of relations with their governors and the authority, but this was not found to be the case, and heads were not slow to express forthright views against the authority or their governors. One unforeseen hazard was that some LEAs and schools were more liable to be visited overmuch by students and research workers, but even CEOs of those authorities which attract more than their fair share of attention, and who asked if it was really necessary to have yet another study there, were very willing to participate. No LEA approached refused to form the subject of a case study. In the ILEA a 50 per cent sample of schools was chosen from within three of the ten administrative divisions, which gave a very representative cross section of the authority, amounting to a 15 per cent sample of all the authority's schools.

There was a standard interview schedule for heads, chairmen of governors and clerks to the governing bodies. In some areas also it was possible to see rank and file governors selected on a random basis. Towards the end of these case studies, which took from two to three weeks, the interviewers met leading members of the education committee for general discussion about the authority's policy on school government, and also saw the CEO and some of his senior officers, mainly to throw light on matters raised in the course of interviews. These interviews were invaluable in producing evidence of very different outlooks on school government, based on criteria of effectiveness and benefit, which were not always apparent to other participants. The accounts and assessments given can fairly be described as free, honest and independent.

A further series of interviews was undertaken for the purpose of observing schemes of school government in transition. The first of these drew on the experience of the London Boroughs, and was devoted to discovering the considerations regarded as important in the formulation of schemes of government by new statutory authorities, and in particular the extent to which existing practices were continued or modified. Interviews were held with CEOs of all the Outer London Boroughs, and in a small follow up study developments which had taken place over the next two years were noted. The other opportunities occurred in two county boroughs were some radical changes had been introduced into the composition or functions of governing bodies with varying success. In both authorities interviews were held with the CEOs and a sample of participants which included heads, councillors and governors.

GAPS AND LIMITATIONS

Some qualifications must be made about the above collection of evidence. The problem of investigating parental opinion on a systematic basis defeated us, and the question of parental participation in school government was examined only in the areas covered by the case studies, although some governors were interviewed whose children attended their own school, and occasional contact was made with members of PTAs or AASEs. While material gathered from these sources cannot be regarded as systematic it is sometimes quite illuminating. With these reservations, the major interests have been covered systematically—although if the study were being planned now it would clearly be necessary to interview a sample of assistant teachers. The rate of non response or refusal to participate strikes us as remarkably low. In the authorities selected for detailed study, involving over one hundred schools, only one head and four governors refused to be interviewed. Replacements were found easily enough on a random basis.

The most extensive enquiry was centred on the LEAs selected for the case studies, which were certainly not a random sample. This lack of typicality is no drawback; the selection of LEAs which appear to take governing bodies seriously is justified by the need to collect material which illustrates the potential of governing bodies in terms of the help and support they give to schools, their influence on members and officers of LEAs and their effectiveness in ensuring lay participation in school government.

The subjective elements in these case studies might limit the

possibility of systematic analysis, if, for example, heads were inclined to exaggerate either the importance or the impotence of
their governing bodies. But it is as essential to find out what heads
or governors feel or think about their functions, as it is to discover
what actually goes on. Any study comparable to our own would
be incomplete if attention were not paid to the participants' own
perceptions and assessments. As it turned out there was no serious
difficulty in reconciling—or in accounting for—the views and attitudes expressed by different participants, and these views and
attitudes themselves were not dependent on isolated incidents
which had left bitter memories. Respondents were concerned to
give as balanced a picture as they could, even when they made it
clear that they had strong views. Where controversies, decisions
or incidents were mentioned, these were discussed in other interviews during the case study. Comparing the accounts of all participants enabled the research staff to judge the situation for
themselves, and thus to discover how far participants shared the
same assumptions, and what conclusions followed from failure to
make these assumptions explicit. Nearly all respondents were very
willing to illustrate the scope (or lack of scope) of governing
bodies from their own experience, often in the most circumstantial
detail. Several respondents, especially among the governors,
could not imagine why they had been selected for attention, and
thought they could make only a routine contribution which would
be of no interest, simply because their experience was not out of
the ordinary; these were balanced by others who thought that it
would be rash and unwarranted to draw any general conclusions
from their own experience which, as some argued with great
force and conviction, was possibly interesting—even fascinating—
but certainly untypical.

THE SCOPE OF THE STUDY

The original objectives of the study were to examine the part
being played in education by governing bodies of county secondary schools, and to suggest the extent to which their functions

might be modified or extended in the light of possible future developments in education and local government. However, from the start there was pressure to expand the project in several directions. As early as September 1965 the Central Advisory Council invited the authors to prepare a paper on Primary School Management for the Plowden Committee. The paper submitted (and subsequently published as Appendix 13 to the Plowden Report) was based on interviews with some 70 CEOs as it was not possible to undertake any further work within the time limit set by the C.A.C. Shortly after work on this paper was completed, the appointment of the Royal Commission on Local Government was announced. The Department of Education and Science readily agreed that the authors should submit to the Royal Commission a full report based on the Unit's first two years' field work. This report gave particular attention to the broader issues concerning school management and government which had been raised in evidence submitted by other bodies to the Royal Commission, and it was decided to concentrate on secondary school government, since primary school management had already been discussed in some measure. The Unit's report was submitted to the Royal Commission in September 1967 and subsequently published as Research Study No. 6.

The third factor was the appointment of the Public Schools Commission. It did not appear that anybody else was giving systematic consideration to the government of independent schools, and a limited study was therefore mounted. The opportunity was used to look at the government of voluntary aided and direct grant schools and LEA boarding schools. A memorandum was submitted to the Commission in January 1968.

Appendix 2: The Literature on School Government

D. A. HOWELL

Writers on English local government, education or social services have given virtually no attention to school governing bodies. Perhaps governing bodies have been no worse treated in this respect than are lay bodies involved in other social services; for example, P. Townsend in his classic work on old people's homes (*The Last Refuge*, 1962) makes no mention at all of management committees of homes maintained by local authorities. The role of the layman in hospital administration receives incidental treatment in H. Eckstein's *The English Health Service*, 1968, pp. 187–8, and J. Carlebach has written (*Caring for Children in Trouble*, 1970, pp. 136–63) rather more fully of the functions of approved school managers, yet the opportunities for lay participation in the social services, which are in theory quite extensive and have been developed as the result of successive governmental policies, do not generally strike writers and commentators as being of major importance in the running of the service.

One might possibly have expected governing and managing bodies to receive more attention from sociological studies of leadership and local groups in English towns or villages. However these either contain nothing at all about managers or governors (e.g. W. M. Williams, *A West Country Village*, 1963, and R. M. Crichton, *Commuters' Village*, 1964) or mention them with the bare minimum of comment, as when Williams in his earlier study (*The Sociology of an English Village*, 1956) remarks dryly (p. 74) 'the social organization of Gosforth is such that it goes on all right without much interference or help from governing bodies'. He does not include managing and governing bodies in a list of formal and informal associations existing in the village. Such negative evidence suggests that, to the outside observer not specifically concerned with education, the impact or influence of governing and managing bodies is insignificant.

It is, of course, usual for descriptions of the English educational system to devote a page or two to the status, composition and functions of governing and managing bodies but no more is generally attempted than a summary account deriving mainly from official sources (see, for example, J. P. Parry, *The Provision of Education in England and Wales*, 1971, and B. Lawrence, *The Administration of Education in Britain*, 1972). Surprisingly, F. Musgrove, in *Patterns of Power and Authority in English Education*, 1971, refers to them only in their historical context. The fullest discussion is found in Derek Birley, *The Education Officer and his World*, 1970, who refers to the role of governing bodies in two places. On pages 41–43, after the usual factual description, he discusses the role of the education officer in what he describes as 'this indistinct and uncertain realm' stressing the series of relationships temporary alliances and regrouping existing between governors, authorities and heads, and also mentions the difficulties arising from sheer weight of numbers and the pressure which this creates for grouped governing bodies. Later on, in an interesting chapter on the education officer and the community (pp. 195–6) Birley suggests that the function actually performed by governors and managers is more important than that of parents. Birley notes that the importance of governors is normally said to reside in certain indefinable functions of a general kind, traditionally concerned with pressing the claims of individual schools against the generalist unfeeling central authority, and protecting heads from the bureaucracy. His conclusions are that the implications of both these functions are in the end negative and therefore likely to be unsatisfying (a view which the authors certainly do not share, at least in respect of the first function). He thinks that recent proposals that the role of governors and managers should be re-defined in terms of the community, acting as a bridge between school and community, and between authority and community has much of value in them, and in this connection makes some important and valuable suggestions. Bridge building is more likely to be achieved by activity than mere membership of committees. More emphasis might be placed on the organizing potential of governors, thereby demonstrating a way in which professionals and interested amateurs can co-operate to make the education service really sensitive to the needs of the community. This could be the first stage in re-interpreting the notion of voluntary service for the present day. There is a need for leaders able to interpret the wishes of the community in relation to the long term plans of the authority, and there is often a need for someone to stand alongside the individual in difficulties and help him find his way through the complexities of the system.

Studies of individual localities by political scientists do not generally give much prominence to governing bodies. Indeed there are only four accounts worth reporting at length. Three of these mention managers and governors incidentally in the context of a broader study of local government or local communities.

A. H. Birch in *Small Town Politics*, 1959, a study of Glossop, points out (pp. 152-3) that the 10 primary schools have 6 managers each, while two secondary schools have 11 governors and the grammar school 20. There are therefore 102 posts variously filled by representatives of the County Council, the Divisional Executive and the Borough Council and, in the case of voluntary schools, by representatives of the churches. In 1955 there 102 appointments were filled by some 70 persons, most of whom were members of the main political parties. Clearly the situation in Glossop was very similar to some of those described later in this study.

Birch's view is that although the system may seem a little cumbersome, it ensures that the people who take decisions are familiar with the practical problems and local feeling. He quotes a primary school in an outlying district which could easily have accommodated twice its existing number of pupils, while another primary school in an adjoining district was overcrowded. As the schools were only half a mile apart, it would have been convenient to transfer some of the pupils but local sentiment was known to have been strongly opposed to such a move, and the Divisional Executive made no attempt to impose it.

This section of Birch's work is not very helpful, since the various elements in the political and administrative structures are not sufficiently distinguished from each other. For example, in the case quoted above, it is not clear what the role of the school managers was as opposed to that of parents or teachers. Moreover there is no discussion of the relationships between managing and governing bodies, the Divisional Executive and the County, except in the most general terms.

Policies and Politics in Secondary Education by D. Peschek and J. A. Brand (LSE, Greater London Papers No. 11, 1966) compares two authorities. Peschek's study of West Ham (pp. 30–4) lists the administrative arrangements, and the general division of functions between the Education Committee and governing bodies. He quotes (pp. 50–2) an incident of interest for the light which it throws on relations between the LEA and the Ministry of Education, as well as between the LEA and the governing body. This centred on an inspection of Stratford Grammar School in 1947 which caused the governing body (which at the time served both the LEAs grammar schools) to be called together to consider the criticisms made. The governors' attention was drawn to deficiencies in accommodation, the relaxed state of school discipline and the unsuitability of both the commerce course and the provision of religious education. The governors decided that the serious inadequacies in accommodation could be overcome only by replacing the school and recommended that the Development Plan be amended to provide an alternative plan. The Ministry replied that the governors made too much of the argument that HMI ignored the damage done by the war and that they should consider whether the existing arrangements provided an adequate daily act of worship for all pupils. The governors however handed the responsibility back in the following terms:

The governors having heard the observations of the Headmaster, recommend that the Minister be informed that they will review the arrangements for religious education, particularly the daily act of worship, when the school is provided in due course with suitable accommodation.

The Ministry was not satisfied and in a further letter to the LEA in July 1948 pointed out the statutory obligations that lay on a school to begin each day with collective worship. It was anxious to know what arrangements the governors proposed to make to improve the quality of the act of worship, and suggested that they might use the dining rooms. The governors dug their heels in and said that existing facilities did not allow collective worship for all pupils at the beginning of every day, but only on alternate days. On their recommendation the LEA told the Ministry that the statutory requirements would be met as soon as the school was provided with an assembly hall.

By the summer of 1949 the governors were 'seriously perturbed' by the lack of an assembly hall, and asked the LEA that priority be given to this item when the 1950 building programme was being considered. Meanwhile the Ministry had decided that it was necessary to exert direct pressure on the LEA and the Minister himself met the Chairman of the Education Committee and the Chairman of the governors. The governors recorded their careful consideration of the Minister's views, and the fight was over when the Head of Stratford Grammar School was instructed:

to make arrangements forthwith for the act of collective worship to be held at the School at the beginning of each school day as required by section 25(1) of the Education Act of 1944 and to submit a report to them at a later meeting on the arrangements made.

The independence shown by the governors and their defiance of the Ministry over a statutory requirement for more than 3 years may be unusual, although not unparalleled, as we see elsewhere; the Ministry was certainly prepared to override local considerations and, apparently to ignore the school's physical limitations in the interest of securing rigid adherence to a national policy.

The description by Brand of school government in Reading (pp. 98-9) in the other half of this study is disappointing, going little further than reciting the formal articles and mentioning only the two stock functions of governors as being to support the Head and to champion the school against the Authority.

A. M. Rees and T. Smith in *Town Councillors*, 1964, give a detailed discussion (pp. 52–4) of the 'patchwork quilt of ancillary activities' undertaken by the councillors of Barking. One has to accept their qualification that too much should not be read into facts relating only to one authority, but area studies have shown that a similar picture to that which they draw can be found in many parts of the country.

The authors point out that in England and Wales at the time of the enquiry each councillor sat on from 3 to 6 main committees, which held an average of 11 meetings a year. The average member would, therefore, have 50 main meetings to attend to a year or approximately one a week. He would moreover have about 143 minor meetings or sub-committee meetings a year, and would in fact attend about 78 per cent of these. In addition his 'homework' might take up to 16 hours a month.

By far the largest category of other posts was that for school governors and managers which accounted for no less than 60 of the total of 123, and only two members of the Council were not governors of schools.

Even though Rees and Smith did not try to evaluate the councillors' subsidiary activities, it is abundantly clear that at that time councillors carried an enormous burden of work, at least in highly urban areas. If all their positions are added together they produce a total of 783, or an average of 26.1 per person. This state of affairs is by no means unparalleled, and must be regarded on all rational grounds as quite staggering.

Finally there is a particularly lively and shrewd account of local government in North East Essex by the editor of the local paper (H. Benham, *Two Cheers for the Town Hall*, 1964). In his account of the local education system (p. 84) Benham discusses how far governing bodies justify the paper work which they entail; and his conclusions might well be supported by many concerned with the administration of education. He describes how, in his letter of appointment, the CEO of Essex told new governors of the desirability of paying occasional visits on ordinary school days, and in particular to the school's morning assembly; he urged an interest in the general condition of the buildings, the standard of heating, lighting and caretaking and the way in which meals are served, and added a list of matters which the Headmaster could settle without reference to the governing body, including the timetable and school examination.

Benham's judgement is that, while managers and governors resolve to make visits, only a minority of them find time and then only in primary schools: 'the great majority soon fall under the spell of the headmaster who is a . . . if they don't'.

New managers and governors may be likely to take their seats intending to act as watchdogs on wasteful expenditure, but after a couple of meetings most are so caught up in the school's needs and are so surprised to discover how much cutting and pruning goes on, that they are proposing and seconding indignant resolutions and protests calling for immediate action on items which the Headmaster knows he will be extremely lucky to get into next year's capital works programme.

Governors are, perhaps, Benham concludes, an insurance against the real abuse, though anything serious is likely to have come to the notice of the LEA officers some time before the governors get wind of it. Their chief use is probably to give as many people as possible a glimpse of what the schools are doing. Whether the governors ever get anywhere near what is really going on in the school depends chiefly on the extent to which the Headmasters feel like taking them into their confidence.

Index